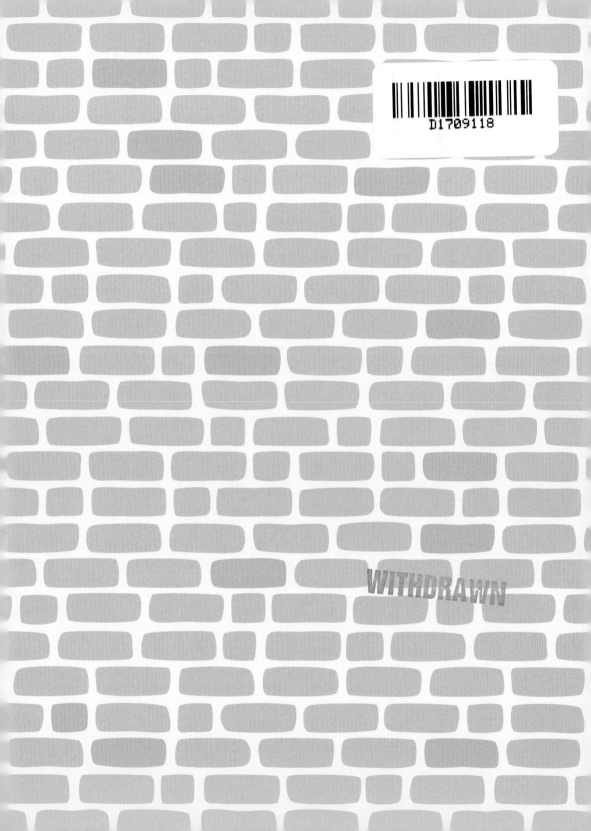

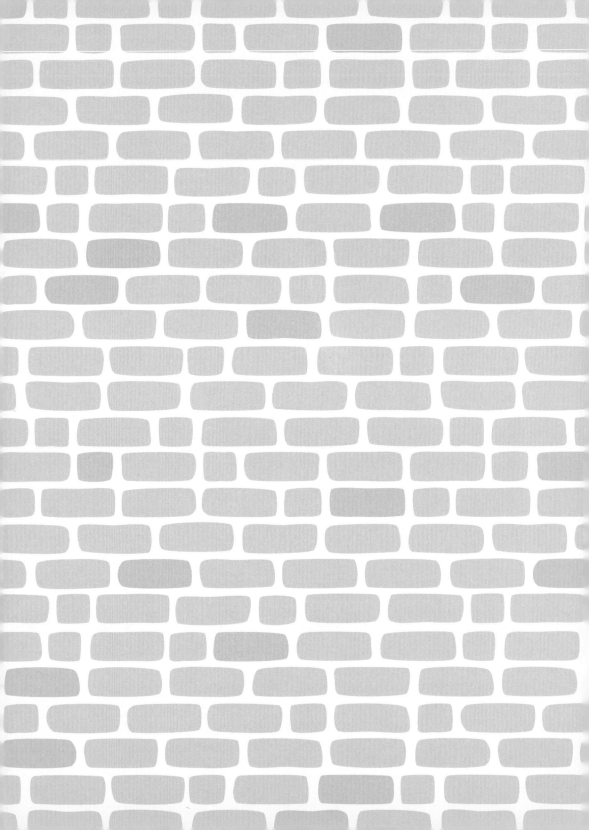

STEAM

⫷ Tales ⫸

The **Wizard** of Oz

L. Frank Baum

Adaptation by Katie Dicker

WELBECK

Published in 2022 by Welbeck Children's Books
An imprint of Welbeck Children's Limited, part of Welbeck Publishing Group
Based in London and Sydney
www.welbeckpublishing.com

The publishers would like to thank the following sources for their kind permission
to reproduce the pictures and footage in this book. The numbers listed below give
the page on which they appear in the book.

Shutterstock (in order of appearance). Vector Tradition 37; Receh Stock 41;
A7880S 41; Incomible 51; Mia Shaly 62; Martin Janecek 65 (left); robin.ph 65
(right); Andrey Korshenkov 65 (bottom); MicroOne 91.

Every effort has been made to acknowledge correctly and contact the source and/or
copyright holder of each picture. Any unintentional errors or omissions will be
corrected in future editions.

ISBN 978 1 78312 846 4

Printed in Dongguan, China

10 9 8 7 6 5 4 3 2 1

FSC
MIX
Paper
FSC® C144853

Author: L. Frank Baum
Adaptation: Katie Dicker
Text and design: Tall Tree Ltd.
Editor: Jenni Lazell
Designer: Sam James
Illustrator: Gustavo Mazali
Production: Melanie Robertson

Contents

Chapter 1

The Twister

It was dull and gray on the day the twister came. Dorothy was an orphan who lived with her Uncle Henry and Aunt Em on a farm in the middle of the great Kansas prairies. Their home was very small with just one room, as the wood used to build it had to be carried for miles. The dry and barren landscape stretched to the horizon all around, without a tree or house in sight.

It was a hard life on the farm. Aunt Em had grown thin and gray, and rarely smiled these days. Uncle Henry worked from dawn to dusk, and barely spoke a word. But Dorothy's little black dog Toto made her laugh and kept her spirits up. They played together for hours, and she loved him dearly.

While Aunt Em was washing the dishes, Uncle Henry and Dorothy looked worriedly at the sky. They heard a low wail of wind from the north, a sharp whistling from the south, and saw ripples running through the grass. "Quick Em, there's a tornado coming," Uncle Henry cried, as he ran to check on the cows and horses. The girls ran for the cellar, but Toto jumped from Dorothy's arms and hid under the bed. Dorothy managed to retrieve him and was just making for the cellar door when a great shriek of wind shook the house so hard that she lost her footing and stumbled to the floor.

WHAT IS A TORNADO?

Tornadoes (or twisters) are powerful swirling storms that form in thunderclouds. When moist, warm air rises and is replaced by cold, dry air, it can sometimes cause the air to spin. As more air moves, the spinning gets faster, a bit like water going down a drain hole. The center or "eye" of the storm is usually calm.

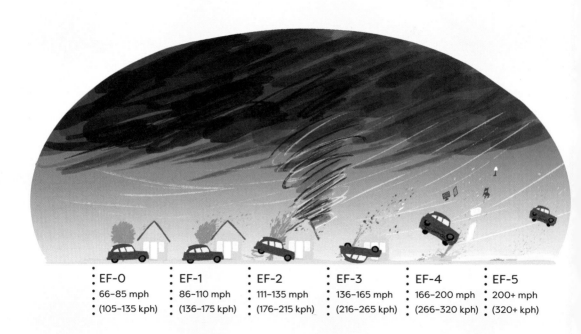

EF-0	EF-1	EF-2	EF-3	EF-4	EF-5
66–85 mph	86–110 mph	111–135 mph	136–165 mph	166–200 mph	200+ mph
(105–135 kph)	(136–175 kph)	(176–215 kph)	(216–265 kph)	(266–320 kph)	(320+ kph)

Tornadoes are measured using the Enhanced Fujita (EF) scale, which ranges from zero to five. At EF-0, winds of up to 85 mph (135 kph) might move roof tiles but at EF-5, winds of more than 200 mph (320 kph) can cause great damage. The worst tornadoes have winds of up to 300 mph (480 kph), strong enough to destroy homes and uproot trees!

Then a strange thing happened. The house whirled around two or three times and rose slowly into the air. The tornado was lifting the house and carrying it away like a feather. Although the wind howled horribly around Dorothy, it was calm in the eye of the storm. Toto barked madly but Dorothy sat quite still on the floor, waiting to see what happened next. As the hours passed, she began to feel sleepy. She crawled to lie on her bed with Toto beside her. Although the house was swaying and the wind was wailing, she soon fell fast asleep.

Dorothy awoke with a shock, so sudden and severe. She realized the house had stopped moving, and bright sunlight was coming through the window. She ran to open the door and gave a cry of amazement at the wonderful sight before her. The tornado had set the house down very gently in the middle of a beautiful country—with rich grass, fruit trees, banks full of flowers, and colorful birds fluttering around. Dorothy was enchanted by a nearby bubbling brook, having lived so long on the dry and dusty prairies.

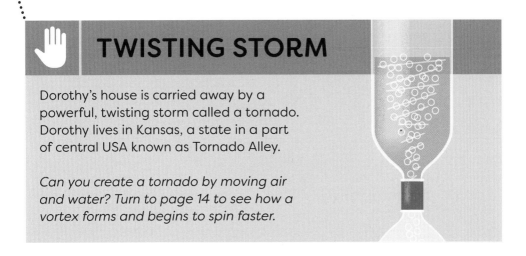

✋ TWISTING STORM

Dorothy's house is carried away by a powerful, twisting storm called a tornado. Dorothy lives in Kansas, a state in a part of central USA known as Tornado Alley.

Can you create a tornado by moving air and water? Turn to page 14 to see how a vortex forms and begins to spin faster.

SLEEP CYCLES

Dorothy sleeps very deeply as the tornado carries her house away. She is only woken when the house reaches the ground again with a jolt.

When we sleep, we go through a series of "sleep cycles," each lasting about 90 minutes. You become drowsy and fall into a light sleep. Then you sink into a deeper sleep, followed by a brief period of light sleep called REM (Rapid Eye Movement). During deep sleep (about 75 percent of our sleep), our body repairs and recharges itself. During light sleep (about 25 percent of our sleep), our brains are more active and we're more likely to dream. Very young children have a shorter sleep cycle (about 45–60 minutes), while older people tend to have a longer period of light sleep.

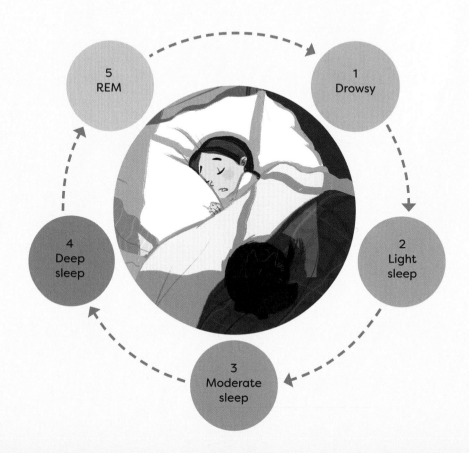

5 REM

1 Drowsy

4 Deep sleep

2 Light sleep

3 Moderate sleep

A small group of people approached—a woman in white and three men dressed in blue. The men were about Dorothy's height, but looked much older. They had pointed hats with bells and the woman wore a gown of glistening stars. The woman bowed low and said in a sweet voice, "You are welcome, most noble Sorceress, to

the land of the Munchkins. Thank you for killing the Wicked Witch of the East, and for setting our people free."

Dorothy couldn't believe what she was hearing. "You're very kind, but there must be some mistake. I haven't killed anything in my life!"

"Your house did, anyway," replied the woman with a laugh. Dorothy gave a little shriek as she noticed two silver shoes sticking out from under the corner beam of the house. "Oh dear! Oh dear! Whatever shall we do?"

"There's nothing to be done," said the woman calmly. "She was the Wicked Witch of the East, who kept all the Munchkins enslaved for many years."

"Are you a Munchkin?" asked Dorothy.

"No, but I'm their friend, the Witch of the North. There are four witches in the Land of Oz. Those of the North and South are good. Now we only fear the Wicked Witch of the West."

The woman went on to describe the wizards who also lived in the Land of Oz. "Oz himself is the Great Wizard," she said. "He's more powerful than the rest of us put together. He lives in the City of Emeralds."

Dorothy was just about to ask a question when the Munchkins gave a loud shout and pointed to the corner of the house. The dead witch's feet had disappeared entirely, leaving just her silver shoes behind.

"She was so old," explained the Witch of the North, "she dried up quickly in the Sun. But the silver shoes are yours." The Munchkins told Dorothy there was an unknown charm connected with the shoes.

"Can you help me find my way?" Dorothy asked. She was anxious to get home to her aunt and uncle who would be looking for her.

The Munchkins and the Witch looked at each other and shook their heads. They explained that a vast desert surrounded the Land of Oz in all directions. "I'm afraid, my dear, that you cannot get home. You'll have to live with us," the woman said softly. And with this Dorothy began to sob, she felt so lonely.

The Witch of the North took off her hat, balanced the point on the end of her nose and counted to three. At once, the hat changed to a slate inscribed with the words "DOROTHY MUST GO TO THE CITY OF EMERALDS."

"Is your name Dorothy, my dear? Then you must go to the City of Emeralds. Perhaps Oz will help you. It's a long journey, but I'll use all the magic I know to keep you safe from harm. And I'll give you my kiss—no one dares hurt someone who's been kissed by the Witch of the North." Her lips left a round, shining mark on Dorothy's forehead.

"The road to the City of Emeralds is paved with yellow brick," continued the Witch, "so you can't miss it. Goodbye, my dear." She whirled around on her left heel three times and disappeared, while the three Munchkins bowed and walked away through the trees.

When she was left alone, Dorothy washed herself and put on her only clean dress—a white and blue gingham check—which was hanging beside her bed, and decided to wear the silver shoes, which fit perfectly.

Filling her basket with bread, she said, "Come along, Toto. We'll go to the Emerald City and ask the Great Oz how to get home again." She locked the door and put the key carefully in her pocket.

It didn't take Dorothy long to find the yellow-brick road and her spirits were lifted by the bright Sun and the sweet singing of the birds. The countryside was so pretty with blue-painted fences by the road, and fields full of grain and vegetables. Whenever she passed a house, the Munchkins came outside to stare and bow before her, knowing she'd destroyed the Wicked Witch and freed them from slavery. The houses were all round and blue, with big domed roofs. This was the country of the East, where blue was the favorite color.

When evening came, Dorothy began to wonder where to spend the night. She walked past a large house, where people were celebrating in the garden. They greeted Dorothy kindly and invited her to eat and stay with them. This was the home of Boq, one of the richest Munchkins in the land. His friends had gathered to celebrate their freedom from the Wicked Witch. "You must be a great sorceress, with your silver shoes and the white in your clothes," Boq said. "Only witches and sorceresses wear white."

"My dress is blue and white,"
Dorothy replied.

"It's kind of you to wear that," said Boq. "Blue is the favored color of the Munchkins, and white is the color of the Witches so we know you must be a friendly witch."

Dorothy didn't know how to respond, for everyone seemed to think she was a witch, when really she was just a little girl.

She slept well that night, with Toto curled up on the blue rug beside her. And after a hearty breakfast, set off again on her travels. "How far is the Emerald City?" she asked Boq.

"I don't know," said Boq gravely, "for I've never been there. I do know that it'll take you many days. The country here is rich and pleasant, but you must pass through rough and dangerous places before you reach the end of your journey."

This worried Dorothy a little, but she knew the Great Oz was the only person who could help her get home again, and so she bravely resolved not to turn back.

RISE AND SHINE

Dorothy is eager to set off after breakfast on her travels to the Emerald City. Sometimes it can be hard to wake early, especially if you've had a long journey!

Perhaps an alarm clock would be useful to Dorothy? Turn to page 16 to discover how to make a simple alarm that stops you from snoozing.

CREATE A TORNADO

Dorothy's house is carried away by a powerful, twisting tornado. Find out how you can create a simple tornado of your own and watch it swirl!

1

Fill two-thirds of one bottle with water. Add a squirt of dishwashing liquid.

YOU WILL NEED:

- 2 empty 2-liter bottles
- water
- dishwashing liquid
- duct tape or tornado tube

2

Hold the empty bottle upside-down on top of the full bottle, with the rims together.

3

Tape the rims together securely using duct tape or a tornado tube. Make sure the seal is water-tight.

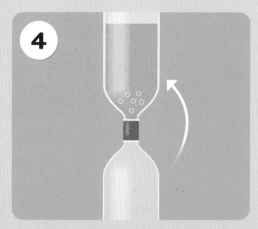

Turn the bottles over, so the full bottle is on top. What do you notice?

Swirl the full bottle quickly in a circular motion. What happens now?

Watch as your tornado swirls and the bubbles replace the water.

WHY IT WORKS

When you turn the bottles over, the air in the bottom bottle stops the water from flowing out. When you swirl the bottle, the air moves up and the water rushes to replace it—a bit like the warm and cold air in a thundercloud. As the water and air move past each other, a twisting vortex forms like a tornado. The tornado also moves faster as the vortex gets narrower.

MAKE AN ALARM

Dorothy wants to set off early on her travels to the Emerald City. Discover how a simple alarm can stop you from snoozing when you want to stay awake!

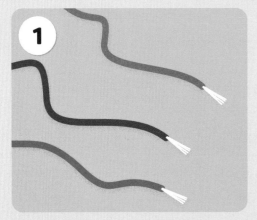

1

Ask an adult to help you take the plastic off the ends of each wire using the wire strippers.

YOU WILL NEED:

- 3 pieces of electrical wire 6 in. (15cm) each
- scissors
- wire strippers
- duct tape
- cardboard
- AA battery, with holder
- buzzer
- silver foil

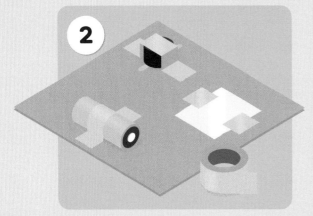

2

Use the duct tape to secure the battery, the buzzer, and a small square of silver foil to a square of cardboard, as shown.

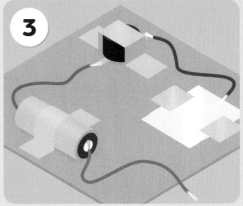

3

Use the wires to attach the buzzer to the battery, the buzzer to the silver foil, and a piece of wire to the other end of the battery. Leave this wire free at the other end.

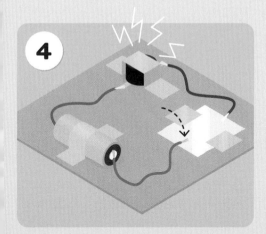

4 Test your buzzer by pressing the end of the free wire onto the silver foil. The buzzer should sound. Check each wire if any are loose.

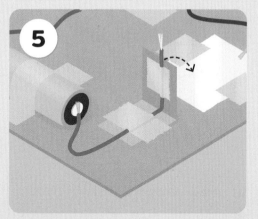

5 Bend the end of the free wire upward slightly. Use duct tape to attach a small piece of cardboard next to the wire to act as a hinge—when the hinge is pressed down, the buzzer should sound.

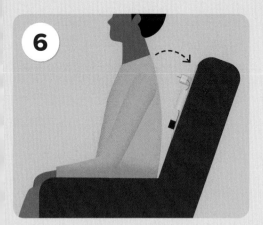

6 Sit down on a chair or sofa and attach your circuit to the back of your chair. When you rest back on the circuit, the buzzer should sound. Now you'll know if you fall asleep!

WHY IT WORKS

Silver foil is a metal that conducts electricity. It can be used as a simple switch to complete the circuit. When you sit back in your chair, the cardboard hinge pushes the wire onto the silver foil to make the buzzer sound. You may be wide awake sitting upright, but if you slouch and doze off, the buzzer will wake you!

Chapter 2

Dorothy to the Rescue

Dorothy continued along the yellow-brick road. After several miles, she stopped to rest and climbed on top of a nearby fence. Beyond lay a great cornfield, with a Scarecrow placed high on a pole to keep away the birds. Its head was a small sack stuffed with straw, with a painted mouth, nose, and eyes. An old, pointed blue hat was perched on its head, and its body was a blue suit, stuffed with straw.

Dorothy was gazing thoughtfully at the Scarecrow when she thought she saw it wink at her. Then a nod of the head! She climbed down and walked toward the Scarecrow, while Toto ran around barking at the pole.

"Good day," said the Scarecrow, in a rather husky voice.

"Did you speak?" asked Dorothy, in wonder.

"Certainly! How do you do?"

"I'm well, thank you," Dorothy replied politely. "How about you?"

"I'm not feeling well," said the Scarecrow, with a smile, "it's very tedious being perched up here day and night to scare away the crows."

"Can't you get down?" asked Dorothy.

"No, this pole is stuck up my back. I'd be so grateful if you could take it away."

Dorothy carefully lifted the Scarecrow off the pole.

"Thank you, I feel like a new man. Who are you?" the Scarecrow asked, "and where are you going?"

"I'm Dorothy, and I'm going to the Emerald City to ask the Great Oz to send me back to Kansas."

"Where's the Emerald City?" he asked. "And who is Oz?"

"Don't you know?" Dorothy remarked, with surprise.

"No, I don't know anything. You see, I'm stuffed, so I have no brains at all," he answered sadly.

"Oh, I'm sorry," said Dorothy.

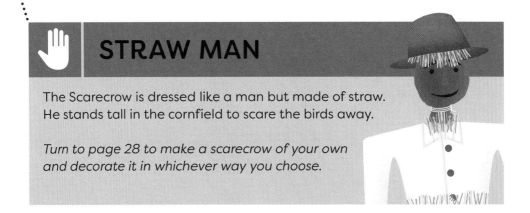

✋ STRAW MAN

The Scarecrow is dressed like a man but made of straw. He stands tall in the cornfield to scare the birds away.

Turn to page 28 to make a scarecrow of your own and decorate it in whichever way you choose.

"Do you think," the Scarecrow asked, "if I go to the Emerald City, Oz will give me some brains?"

"I don't know, but you can come with me if you like. If Oz can't give you any brains, you'll be no worse off than you are now."

"That's true," said the Scarecrow. "I don't mind my body being stuffed because I can't feel pain. But I don't want people to call me a fool."

"I understand how you feel," said Dorothy. "If you come with me, I'll ask Oz to do all he can for you." And with that, they set off together on the yellow-brick road.

Toto was suspicious of the Scarecrow at first. "Don't mind Toto," Dorothy said to her new friend. "He never bites."

"Oh, I'm not afraid," replied the Scarecrow. "He can't hurt the straw. Do let me carry your basket for you, since I can't get tired either! In fact, there's only one thing in the world I'm afraid of—a lit match."

After a few hours, the road became rough. The Scarecrow kept tripping over, but it didn't hurt him. There were fewer houses and fruit trees here, and the farther they went, the more dismal things became. At noon, they rested by a little brook. Dorothy offered the Scarecrow some bread, but he explained he never got hungry.

FALLING SAFELY

The Scarecrow doesn't hurt himself when he falls because he has no nerves to feel pain, no muscles to pull, nor limbs to break.

We all fall over from time to time, but there are things we can do to fall safely. Relaxing is key. Instead of tensing up, try to fall with relaxed, bent elbows and knees to lessen the impact. Rolling when you fall will also spread the impact over a larger part of your body. If you fall forward, turn your head to the side to protect your face and nose. If you fall backward, tuck your chin in to lift your head away from the floor. Always try to fall on your bottom or thigh, instead of your limbs. You're less likely to sprain or break a bone this way. You may bruise, but it will soon heal!

Relax your arms to absorb your fall.

Turn as you fall to protect your head and face.

As you roll, you can place your arms palm down to stop you.

"Tell me something about yourself and the country you came from," said the Scarecrow, when she'd finished eating. So, Dorothy told him all about Kansas and how gray everything was there, and how the tornado had carried her to this strange Land of Oz.

"I can't understand why you'd wish to leave this beautiful country and go back to the dry, gray place you call Kansas," the Scarecrow said.

"That's because you have no brains," replied Dorothy. "No matter how gray our homes are, my family live there—there's no place like home."

The Scarecrow sighed, "Of course, I cannot understand it."

"Won't you tell me a story, while we're resting?" Dorothy asked.

The Scarecrow looked sad. "I was only made the day before yesterday. I remember the farmer painted my ears first and then my eyes. When he walked away, I tried to follow, but my feet didn't touch the ground. It was a lonely life with nothing to think of. Whenever birds flew away scared, it made me feel like an important person. Then an old crow wasn't fooled by me and boldly ate all the corn he wanted. The other birds followed. I felt I wasn't a good Scarecrow after all, but the crow said if only I had brains, I'd be as good a man as any."

Dorothy and the Scarecrow set off once more. There were no fences by the roadside now and the land was rough. As evening approached, they came to a great forest, where the trees grew so close together, their branches met over the road. It was almost dark under the trees, but the travelers didn't stop.

After an hour, the light faded, and they found themselves stumbling in the dark. Dorothy couldn't see at all, but Toto and the Scarecrow led the way. "If you see somewhere to spend the night, you must tell me," Dorothy said. "It's very uncomfortable walking in the dark!"

Soon after, the Scarecrow stopped. "There's a little wooden cottage to the right of us," he said. "Let's go there."

The Scarecrow led her to the cottage, where they found a bed of dried leaves. Dorothy and Toto lay down at once, and soon fell sound asleep. The Scarecrow, who was never tired, waited patiently until morning.

When Dorothy woke, the Sun was shining through the trees and Toto had been out chasing squirrels. The Scarecrow was still standing patiently in the corner. "We must find water to wash and to drink," she said.

They left the cottage and walked through the trees until they found a little brook, where Dorothy drank and bathed and ate her breakfast. Just as they were about to embark on the yellow-brick road again, Dorothy was startled to hear a deep groan nearby.

"What was that?" she asked timidly.

Then another groan. The sound seemed to come from behind them. They walked back a few steps when they saw something shining in the sunlight. One of the big trees had been chopped through, and standing beside it, with an uplifted axe in his hands, was a man made entirely of tin! He stood perfectly still.

Dorothy and the Scarecrow looked in amazement, while Toto barked.

"Did you groan?" asked Dorothy.

"Yes," answered the Tin Man. "I've been groaning for more than a year, and no one has ever come to my aid."

"What can I do for you?" Dorothy asked softly.

"Could you get an oil-can for my joints?" he said. "They've rusted so badly I can't move at all. You'll find an oil-can in my cottage."

Dorothy ran back to the cottage at once and returned with the oil-can. "Where are your joints?" she asked anxiously.

 ## RUST REACTIONS

The Tin Man has to avoid getting wet so he doesn't seize up. His salty tears are even worse.

What is it about water, salt, and metal that causes such havoc? Turn to page 30 to make some rust reactions of your own and discover the conditions that make metals corrode.

WHY DOES RUST FORM?

Rust forms when a metal, such as iron, combines with water and oxygen in a process called oxidation.

Iron, for example, forms iron oxide (rust) when it's exposed to moisture in the air. If a metal continues to oxidize, it's a form of corrosion and the metal wears away. You may notice that a car rusts in places where the paintwork has become worn.

Paint is a good rust protector because it keeps the air (oxygen) away. Salt water causes metal to corrode five times faster than fresh water. If you live by the sea, you'll notice a lot more rust around you!

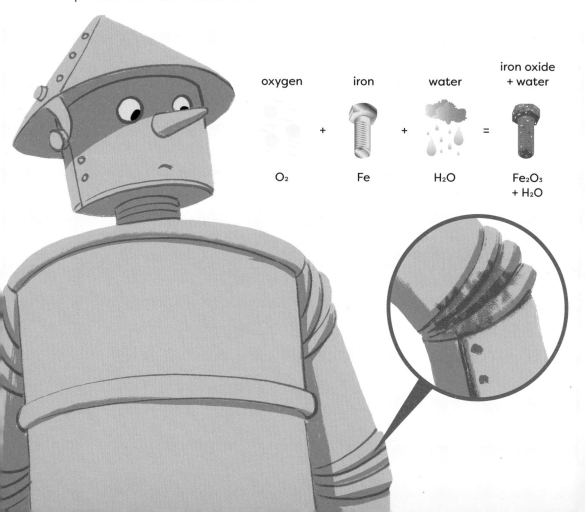

oxygen   iron   water   iron oxide + water

O_2 +   Fe   + H_2O = Fe_2O_3 + H_2O

"Oil my neck, first," replied the Tin Man. It was quite badly rusted so while Dorothy oiled it, the Scarecrow moved the head gently from side to side until it moved freely and the Tin Man could turn it himself.

"Now my arms," he said. Once they'd repeated the process, the Tin Man gave a sigh of relief and lowered his axe, which he leaned against the tree. "If you could just oil my legs, I'll be all right once more." He kept thanking them and seemed a very polite creature.

"I might have stood there forever if you hadn't come along," he said, "so you've certainly saved my life. What brought you here?"

"We're on our way to the Emerald City to see Oz," Dorothy said.

"Why do you wish to see Oz?" he asked.

"I want him to send me back to Kansas, and the Scarecrow would like some brains," she replied.

The Tin Man thought deeply for a moment. "Do you suppose Oz could give me a heart?"

"I guess so," Dorothy replied. "If he can give the Scarecrow brains."

"Well if you'd allow me to join your party, I'll ask Oz for help."

"Come along," said the Scarecrow and Dorothy warmly. They put the oil-can in Dorothy's basket in case the Tin Man got caught in the rain and rusted, and the three of them passed through the forest to find the yellow-brick road again.

MAKE A SCARECROW

The Scarecrow is dressed in straw-stuffed clothes and stands tall in the field on a pole. Learn how to make a scarecrow of your own to frighten away the birds!

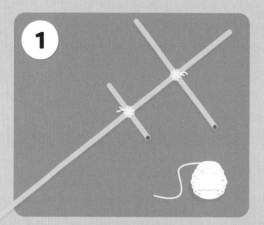

1

Tie the two longest sticks together to make a cross shape for the body and arms, as shown. Tie the other stick horizontally as well, about halfway down.

YOU WILL NEED:

- 3 sticks or bamboo canes, about 6.5 feet, 3 feet, and 16 inches (2 m, 1 m and 40 cm) long
- old clothes (such as trousers, shirt and hat)
- pair of old tights
- string • scissors • paints
- straw or leaves

2

Cut one leg from the tights and fill it with straw to make a firm head shape. Tie with string to secure.

3

Paint the eyes, nose and mouth onto the scarecrow's head. You could add some ears, a beard, or a mustache if you want.

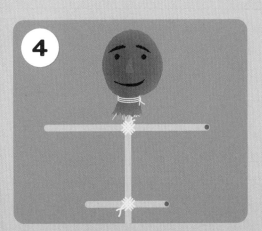

4 Tie the head to the top of the frame. You could put the stick inside the head to make it more secure.

5 Hang the shirt around the arms of the scarecrow frame and button it up. Hang the trousers from the crossbar. Stuff them with straw and tie the ends with string to secure.

6 Put some straw inside the hat and place it on the scarecrow's head. Leave some straw hanging down to look like hair. Put your scarecrow outside to see if he scares away the birds!

WHY IT WORKS

Scarecrows have been used for centuries to scare birds away from farmers' fields. At first, the farmers did this job themselves, but they soon used scarecrows to replace them. Some farmers tie metal objects to the arms to make a noise as well. Others use the moving reflective surface of a hanging CD to distract a bird's vision and scare it away.

RUST REACTIONS

The Tin Man has to be careful with his salty tears.
Discover how oxygen and water cause metal to rust,
and how salt can make things worse!

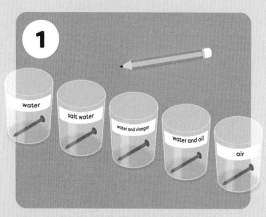

1

water | salt water | water and vinegar | water and oil | air

YOU WILL NEED:

- 5 small beakers
- 5 iron nails
- pen
- notepad
- sticky labels
- water
- salt
- vinegar
- cooking oil

Put an iron nail in each of the beakers and place them in a line. Label them as follows: water; salt water; water and vinegar; water and oil; air.

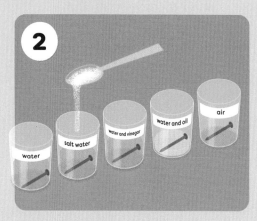

2

water | salt water | water and vinegar | water and oil | air

Fill four of the beakers with the following liquids: ⅓ cup (100 ml) water; ⅓ cup (100 ml) water with 1 tsp salt; ⅓ cup (100 ml) water with 1 tsp vinegar; 1 tbsp cooking oil. Leave the fifth beaker empty.

3

water and oil

Take the beaker with cooking oil and add ⅓ cup (100 ml) of water. What do you notice about the oil?

4

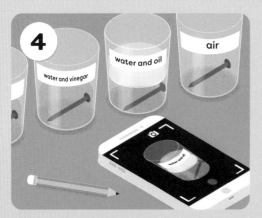

Check the beakers each day and write down your observations. You could take photos to record your findings.

5

Keep recording your findings over a period of three weeks. What do you notice happening as the days go by?

6

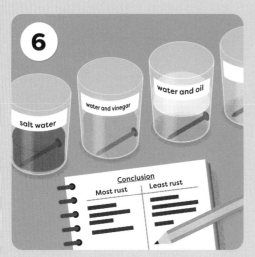

Write down the conclusions of your experiment. Which conditions cause the most rust? Which conditions cause the least?

WHY IT WORKS

You should find that the nails in water rust first. When salt is added to water, the reaction goes faster. The water with vinegar will corrode too, but only some of this corrosion is visible as rust. The beaker with oil will show no rust. Oil and water don't mix, so the oil forms a protective barrier, keeping oxygen away from the nail. The beaker of air may show some rust if the air is full of moisture.

Chapter 3

The Cowardly Lion

Soon, the trees and branches grew so thick that the Tin Man had to use his axe to clear a passage. The Scarecrow stumbled into a hole. "Why didn't you walk around the hole?" asked the Tin Man.

"I don't know how to avoid the holes," the Scarecrow replied. "My head is full of straw and that's why I want to ask Oz for some brains."

"Brains aren't the best thing in the world," the Tin Man remarked.

"Do you have any?" asked the Scarecrow.

"No, my head's empty," replied the Tin Man. "But once I had brains, and a heart. Having tried them both, I'd much rather have a heart."

"And why's that?" asked the Scarecrow.

"I'll tell you my story," the Tin Man continued. "My father was a woodman and when I grew up, I became a woodman too. When my parents died, I thought I'd marry, instead of living alone.

"There was a beautiful Munchkin girl I loved with all my heart. She lived with an old woman who didn't want her to marry me—she was so lazy she wanted the girl to stay and do the cooking and cleaning.

"The old woman promised the Wicked Witch of the East two sheep and a cow if she could stop the marriage. The Witch enchanted my axe, and when I was chopping wood, the axe cut off my left leg. I asked a tinsmith to make a new leg from tin. When I started chopping again, my axe cut off my right leg. And so it went on. Each time I replaced a body part with tin, the axe would cut off another.

"When the tinsmith replaced my head, I thought I'd beaten the Wicked Witch. I worked hard to build our first home. But she thought of a new way to kill my love—this time the axe cut right through my body. The tinsmith made a body of tin, but I had no heart, so I lost my love for the Munchkin girl and didn't care whether I married her or not.

"By this point, it didn't matter if my axe slipped because it couldn't cut me. The only danger was my joints rusting, so I kept an oil-can. One day, I forgot the oil and was caught in a rainstorm, which rusted my joints and stopped me from moving. I stood there for a whole year, and realized the greatest loss I'd known was the loss of my heart. When I was in love, I was the happiest man in the world. I'd like Oz to give me a heart, so I can go back to the Munchkin girl and marry her."

All this time they'd been walking through the thick woods. The yellow-brick road was covered with dried branches and dead leaves, which made it difficult to walk. A few birds were singing, but now and then a deep growl could be heard nearby. Dorothy's heart began to beat faster.

"How long will it take to get out of the forest?" Dorothy asked.

"I don't know," the Tin Man replied, "for I've never been to the Emerald City. My father went once. He said it was a long journey through a dangerous country. But we needn't be afraid. Nothing can hurt the Scarecrow. I'm okay if I have my oil-can, and the mark of the Good Witch's kiss on your forehead will protect you from harm."

"But what about Toto?" Dorothy asked anxiously.

"We must protect him ourselves," the Tin Man replied.

Just then, a roar came from the forest, and a Lion bounded up. With a blow of his paw, he sent the Scarecrow tumbling. Then he struck the Tin Man with his claws but to his surprise, he made no scratches.

Toto ran barking at the Lion, and the beast opened his mouth to bite the dog. Dorothy rushed forward and slapped the Lion on the nose as hard as she could. "Don't you dare bite Toto!" she cried. "You ought to be ashamed of yourself, a big beast like you, to bite a poor little dog!"

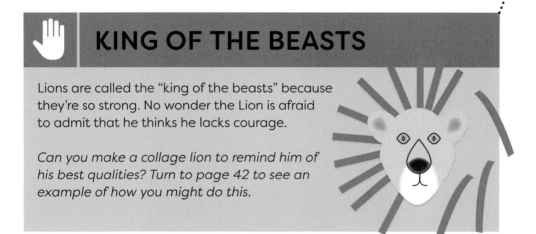

KING OF THE BEASTS

Lions are called the "king of the beasts" because they're so strong. No wonder the Lion is afraid to admit that he thinks he lacks courage.

Can you make a collage lion to remind him of his best qualities? *Turn to page 42 to see an example of how you might do this.*

"I didn't bite him," said the Lion, as he rubbed his nose with his paw.

"No, but you tried to," she replied. "You're nothing but a big coward."

"I am," said the Lion in shame. "But what can I do?"

"I don't know," Dorothy continued, "but to think that you struck a stuffed man like the poor Scarecrow!"

"Is he stuffed?" asked the Lion in surprise.

"Of course he's stuffed," replied Dorothy, who was still angry.

"That's why he went over so easily," remarked the Lion. "Is the other one stuffed, too?"

"No," said Dorothy, "he's made of tin."

"That's why he nearly blunted my claws," said the Lion. "And what about that little animal you're so fond of? Is he made of tin, or stuffed?"

"Neither, he's a dog," Dorothy said.

"Oh! No one would think of biting such a little thing, except a coward like me," said the Lion sadly.

"What makes you a coward?" asked Dorothy, looking at the great beast.

MOHS HARDNESS SCALE

The Lion tries to scratch the Tin Man with his claws but he doesn't make a mark. "Hardness" is a property used to describe the way in which some materials resist being bent, scratched, or squashed.

Scientists use different scales to measure the hardness of materials. Metals are often measured using the Vickers test, while minerals are measured using the Mohs scale. The hardest known material on Earth is diamond. For this reason, diamond tips are used extensively in industry to cut or grind other hard surfaces.

Increasing Hardness →

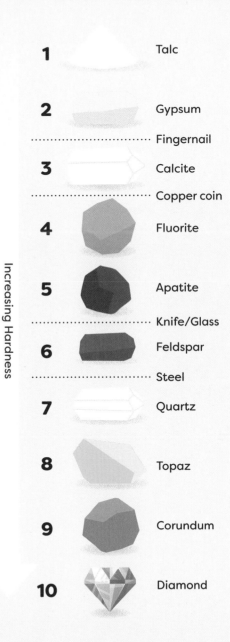

1	Talc
2	Gypsum
	Fingernail
3	Calcite
	Copper coin
4	Fluorite
5	Apatite
	Knife/Glass
6	Feldspar
	Steel
7	Quartz
8	Topaz
9	Corundum
10	Diamond

"It's a mystery," replied the Lion. "I suppose I was born that way. All the other animals expect me to be brave. I learned that if I roared loudly, every living thing was frightened and got out of my way."

"But the King of the Beasts shouldn't be a coward," remarked the Scarecrow.

"I know," replied the Lion. "It's my greatest sorrow and makes me very unhappy."

The travelers explained why they were going to visit the Great Oz in the City of Emeralds.

"Do you think Oz could give me courage?" asked the Cowardly Lion.

"There's no reason why not," said Dorothy.

"Then if you don't mind, I'll go with you," said the Lion. "For my life is simply unbearable without courage."

"You'll be very welcome," replied Dorothy, "for you'll keep away wild beasts. It seems to me they must be more cowardly than you, if they're scared so easily."

They camped that night under a large tree in the forest, before setting off again at sunrise. They'd only been walking an hour when they came to a great deep ditch across the road, which divided the forest. The sides were steep and there were big, jagged rocks at the bottom.

"What shall we do?" asked Dorothy despairingly.

"We can't fly or climb down," the Scarecrow said. "If we can't jump over it, we'll have to stop."

"I think I could jump over it," said the Lion, looking at the distance very carefully.

"You could carry us all over on your back, one at a time," the Scarecrow suggested. "Why don't I go first? I won't be hurt if I fall."

The Scarecrow sat on the Lion's back and with a great leap, the Lion landed safely on the other side. The group were delighted as he carried them over one by one, before resting.

The forest on the other side was very dark and gloomy and they wondered if they'd ever reach bright sunlight again. There were strange noises and the Lion whispered that Kalidahs were found in this part of the country. "They're monstrous beasts with bodies like bears and heads like tigers," he explained, "with claws so long and sharp, they could tear me in two. I'm terribly afraid of the Kalidahs."

"I'm not surprised, they sound dreadful," Dorothy added.

The Lion was about to reply when they came to another great ditch across the road. This one was so broad and deep the Lion knew he couldn't leap across it. "If the Tin Man can chop that great tree down so it falls to the other side," the Scarecrow suggested, "we could walk across it like a bridge."

"That's an excellent idea," said the Lion. "One would almost suspect you had brains!"

The Tin Man set to work at once, and the Lion put his strong front legs against the tree to help it fall. They'd just started to cross, when a sharp growl startled them, and to their horror there were two great beasts with bodies like bears and heads like tigers. "Kalidahs!" cried the Lion, beginning to tremble. "Quick!" cried the Scarecrow. "Let's cross!"

BUILDING BRIDGES

The wooden tree trunk is a useful bridge to cross the ditch. Whenever engineers build a bridge, they must think about the materials they use and the design they take.

Can you make a paper bridge that carries a load? Turn to page 44 to test the different qualities of varying bridge designs.

BRIDGE DESIGNS

Every time a bridge is made, there are different engineering challenges. A bridge needs supports to hold it up. It also needs to be strong enough to carry a load.

There are six basic bridge designs:

Beam
Simple horizontal beam with regular supports. Good for short distances.

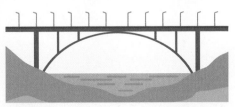

Arch
Curved structure, which spreads the load outward. Good for longer distances.

Truss
Rigid structure with triangular sections. Strong and good for heavy loads.

Cantilever
Rigid structure for heavy loads. Good for uneven foundations.

Suspension
Horizontal deck hung from suspension cables. Towers at each end support the weight. Can span long distances.

Cable-stayed
Horizontal deck supported by towers and diagonal cables. Good for distances longer than cantilever but shorter than suspension.

MAKE A COLLAGE LION

The Lion says he lacks courage, but he has many other qualities. Create your own lion collage to show some important characteristics that someone can have.

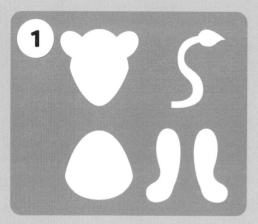

1

Use this simple template as a guide to draw and cut out shapes for the lion's body, legs, head, and tail from pieces of colored paper.

YOU WILL NEED:

- sheet of printer paper
- colored paper
- old magazines or newspapers
- scissors • glue
- pencil, colored pencils, or pens

2

Draw eyes, nose, and a mouth on your lion's head.

3

Cut strips of colored paper about 4 inches (10 cm) long for your lion's mane. Stick these to the back of the head.

4

Glue the different parts of your lion to the printer paper.

5

Decorate your lion with words that describe his qualities, such as "brave" and "fierce." You could cut words out of magazines or newspapers to help you.

6

Use the pencils or pens to add a background (such as the African savanna) and display your lion in a prominent position!

WHY IT WORKS

Lions are called the "king of the beasts" because they're so strong. A lion's body is mostly made of muscle, with very little fat. They can run up to 50 miles per hour (80 kph) over a short distance and their roar can be heard 5 miles (8 km) away! Lions also have powerful jaws with long, sharp teeth, and long, retractable claws.

BUILD A PAPER BRIDGE

The Scarecrow suggests using a strong tree trunk as a bridge. He knows the wood will support their weight. Build some bridges of your own to see which are up to the challenge!

1

Stack the books, two on each side, with a gap between them.

YOU WILL NEED:

- 4 books, all the same thickness
- 3 pieces of paper
- tape
- string
- plastic cup
- hole punch
- coins (of the same size)

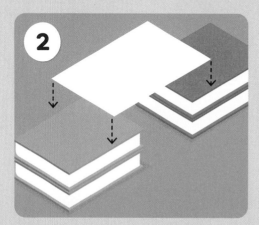

2

Place one sheet of paper on top of the books, as shown. Does it sag or stay straight?

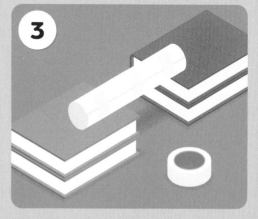

3

Now roll some paper into a tube and tape securely. Place this "bridge" over the books. Does it sag or stay straight?

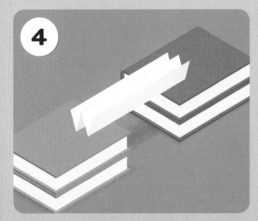

4

This time, fold some paper in half lengthways, then fold back the two sides to create a "W" shape, as shown. Place this "bridge" over the books. Does it sag or stay straight?

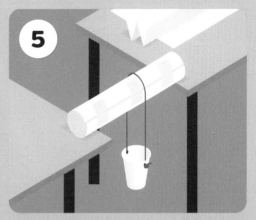

5

Put your bridges between two tables (or similar). Ask an adult to punch two holes in the plastic cup. Use the string to attach the cup to each bridge as shown.

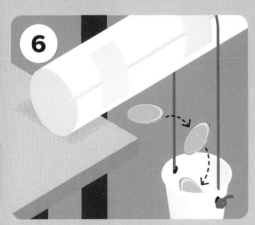

6

Add coins, one at a time. Which bridge withstands the most weight? Make a record of your findings.

WHY IT WORKS

A flat piece of paper tends to sag because it is so thin. If you roll the paper, you increase the thickness over a small area. What shapes do you notice around you that have a similar design—perhaps the metal tubes of a table or chair leg? The folded bridge can also take more coins because the weight is spread out over a wider area. What everyday materials have folds and why are they used? Think of corrugated cardboard, for example.

Chapter 4

Danger All Around

Dorothy crossed the bridge first, holding Toto, and the Tin Man and Scarecrow followed. The Lion turned to face the Kalidahs and gave a terrible roar, which made Dorothy scream and the Scarecrow fall over. The Kalidahs stopped and looked at him in surprise.

But they were much bigger than the Lion and there were two of them. As they rushed forward, the Lion turned to Dorothy, "Stand close behind me, and I'll fight them as long as I can."

"Wait!" said the Scarecrow, and he asked the Tin Man to chop away the end of the tree. Just as the Kalidahs were nearly across, the tree fell with a crash into the ditch, carrying the ugly snarling brutes with it.

"Thank goodness," said the Lion, drawing a huge sigh of relief.

The travelers were anxious to leave the forest and set off at a rapid pace. Dorothy soon tired and rode on the Lion's back. To their great joy, the trees became thinner and by afternoon, they came to a wide river. They could see the yellow-brick road on the other side.

"How shall we cross the river?" Dorothy asked.

"The Tin Man must build a raft," replied the Scarecrow.

The Tin Man gathered wood, while the Scarecrow picked fruit from a nearby tree. Dorothy had eaten nothing but nuts all day and was grateful for the feast. The raft took some time to build, and when night came they settled under the trees. Dorothy dreamed of the Emerald City, and of Oz, who would soon send her back home again.

The next morning, they set off on the raft. Dorothy sat in the middle with Toto. Soon they were all on board, and the Scarecrow and Tin Man used long poles to push them through the water.

They were making good progress when a swift current in the middle of the river swept the raft downstream, and the water grew so deep, the long poles wouldn't touch the bottom.

"This is bad," said the Tin Man. "If we can't get to land, we'll be carried to the country of the Wicked Witch of the West."

The Scarecrow pushed so hard on his long pole that it stuck fast in the riverbed. Before he could pull it out again—or let go—the raft was swept away, and the poor Scarecrow was left clinging to the pole.

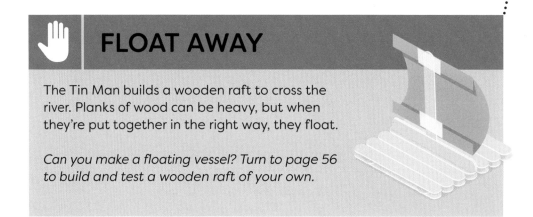

✋ FLOAT AWAY

The Tin Man builds a wooden raft to cross the river. Planks of wood can be heavy, but when they're put together in the right way, they float.

Can you make a floating vessel? Turn to page 56 to build and test a wooden raft of your own.

RIVER CURRENTS

Currents are fast-moving channels of water.

They are difficult to swim or sail against. In a river, the water rushes downstream because it is pulled by the force of gravity. A river's current depends on the amount of water in the river, the steepness of the river, and any interruptions in the riverbed, such as rocks or basins. When a river runs straight, the current is faster in the middle than at the edges. In a meandering river, the current is fastest along the outside bend, and slowest on the inside bend.

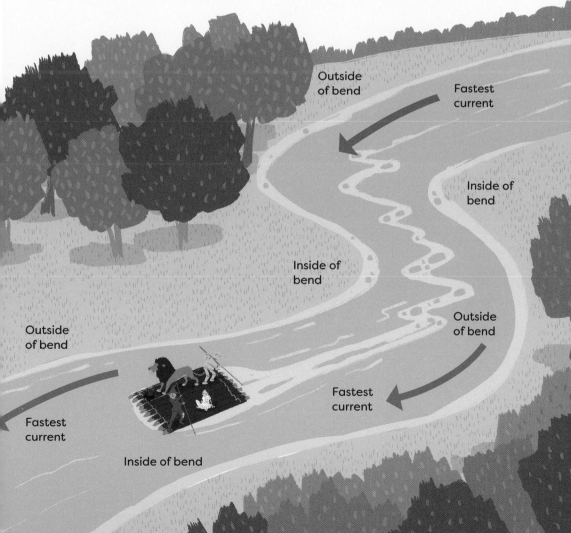

Outside of bend

Fastest current

Inside of bend

Inside of bend

Outside of bend

Outside of bend

Fastest current

Fastest current

Inside of bend

"I'm now worse off than when I first met Dorothy," the Scarecrow thought. "I'm afraid I'll never have any brains, after all!"

The rest of the party floated downstream. "I think I can swim to shore and pull the raft after me if you hold tightly to the tip of my tail," the Lion said.

He sprang into the water and began to swim with all his might toward the shore. It was hard work, but they were slowly drawn out of the current, and Dorothy used the Tin Man's long pole to help push the raft to land.

They were all tired when they reached the shore and lay on the soft grass to rest. The stream had carried them a long way from the yellow-brick road. "We must walk along the riverbank until we reach the road again," the Lion said.

As they set off through the flowers and fruit trees, they would have been content in the sunshine, were they not feeling sorry for the Scarecrow. Before long they could see him perched upon his pole in the middle of the river, looking very lonely indeed.

"What can we do to save him?" Dorothy asked.

The Lion and Tin Man shook their heads sorrowfully and gazed wistfully at the Scarecrow. Meanwhile, a Stork flew by and stopped at the water's edge. "Who are you and where are you going?" she asked.

FLOATING

It's hard to imagine that a huge tanker ship could possibly float in the ocean. How can such a heavy vessel stay on top of the water?

The secret is something called buoyancy. An object floats when its weight is balanced by the weight of the water it displaces. This is why a small stone sinks to the bottom of the ocean, but a wide, heavy ship floats on the surface. Different objects float at different levels under the water. When an object is lowered onto the water, the upward force of the water increases until the forces become balanced. We call this balance equilibrium.

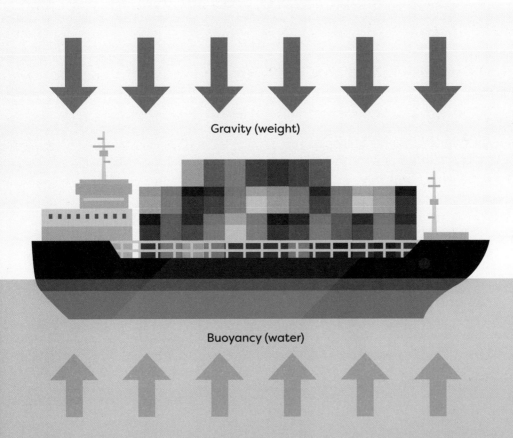

Gravity (weight)

Buoyancy (water)

"I'm Dorothy and these are my friends. We're going to the Emerald City, but we've lost the Scarecrow, and we're wondering how to get him back," Dorothy pointed to the Scarecrow's position.

"If he wasn't so big, I'd get him for you," the Stork remarked.

"He isn't heavy at all!" Dorothy said eagerly. "He's stuffed with straw, and if you'll bring him back to us, we'll be so grateful."

"I'll try," said the Stork, "but if he's too heavy, I'll have to drop him."

The Stork flew off and grabbed the Scarecrow by the arm with her great claws and carried him back to land. The Scarecrow was so happy to be among his friends again, he hugged them all.

"I was afraid I'd have to stay in the river forever," he said. "Thank you, Stork."

"That's alright," said the Stork. "I always like to help anyone in trouble. But I must go now. I hope you'll find the Emerald City and that Oz will help you."

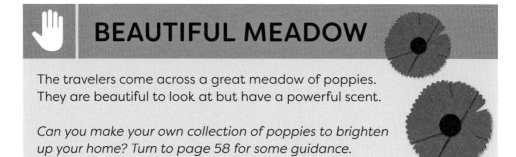

✋ BEAUTIFUL MEADOW

The travelers come across a great meadow of poppies. They are beautiful to look at but have a powerful scent.

Can you make your own collection of poppies to brighten up your home? Turn to page 58 for some guidance.

The travelers walked on through the beautiful countryside. Occasionally there were great clusters of scarlet poppies that almost dazzled Dorothy's eyes. "Aren't they beautiful!" she said, as she breathed in their spicy scent. Soon they found themselves in the middle of a great meadow of poppies. Their smell was so powerful that they made Dorothy want to lie down and rest. Before long, she found herself unable to keep her eyes open, and she fell among the poppies, fast asleep.

"What shall we do?" asked the Tin Man.

"If we leave her here, she'll die," said the Lion. "The smell of the flowers is killing us all. I can scarcely keep my eyes open, and Toto is asleep already."

The Scarecrow and Tin Man were unaffected by the powerful scent. "Run fast," the Scarecrow said to the Lion, "and get out as soon as you can. We'll bring Dorothy with us, but make sure you don't fall asleep, as you're too big to be carried."

The Lion bounded off, while the Scarecrow and Tin Man carried Dorothy and Toto. At last, they came upon the Lion slumped fast asleep in the poppies. He'd fallen only a short distance from the sweet grass that spread into beautiful fields beyond.

"We can't save him," the Tin Man said sadly, "he's much too heavy to lift. Perhaps he'll dream he's found courage at last."

They carried Dorothy to a pretty spot beside the river and laid her gently on the soft grass where the fresh breeze could wake her.

"We can't be far from the yellow-brick road now," said the Scarecrow. The Tin Man was just about to reply when a low growl revealed a strange beast bounding over the grass toward them. It was a great yellow Wildcat chasing a little gray field mouse. Although the Tin Man had no heart, he knew it was wrong for the Wildcat to kill such a harmless creature, so he intervened.

"Oh, thank you for saving my life!" the little mouse said in a squeaky voice. "You've done a great deed in saving me. I'm the Queen of all the Field Mice." At that moment, several mice were seen running up as fast as their little legs could carry them.

"This Tin Man saved my life," the Queen explained. "You must all serve him and obey his every wish."

"Is there anything we can do to repay your kindness," one of the biggest mice asked. At which the Scarecrow replied, "Oh, yes! You can help save our friend the Lion who's asleep in the poppy field."

"A Lion!" cried the Queen with fright.

"Don't worry, he's a coward and he'd never hurt anyone who's our friend. If you help us to save him, I promise he'll treat you well."

The Scarecrow asked if the mice could gather all their friends, and each bring a long piece of string. He asked the Tin Man to make a wooden truck to carry the Lion. Thousands of mice returned from all directions and the Scarecrow and Tin Man fastened them to the truck so they could use their combined strength to pull it quite easily. After a great deal of hard work, they managed to lift the Lion and roll him out of the poppy field.

By this time Dorothy had woken and thanked the mice warmly for saving her friend. As they scampered off, the Queen said, "If you ever need us again, just call us with this whistle. We shall hear you and come to your aid. Goodbye!"

They all sat down with relief and feasted on some nearby fruit while they waited for the Lion to wake up.

MAKE A RAFT

The Tin Man builds a wooden raft to cross the river. Try building a wooden raft of your own and test how well it floats in water.

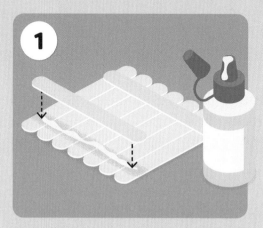

1

Lay 7 wooden craft sticks side by side. Glue 2 wooden craft sticks horizontally across, as shown, to secure them.

YOU WILL NEED:

- 19 wooden craft sticks
- glue gun or tube of glue
- tape
- 6 x 8-inch (A5 size) sheet of paper
- scissors

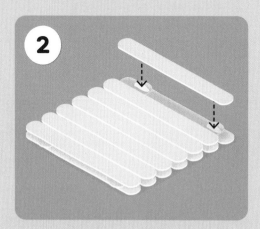

2

Add 7 more wooden craft sticks to the other side for a strong shape.

3

Take the last 3 wooden craft sticks. Glue them together in a T shape, as shown, to make a mast.

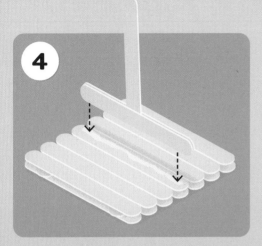

4

Glue your mast to the raft, with the top of the T facing down.

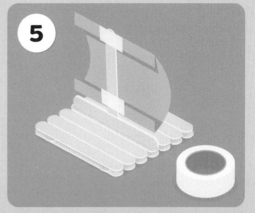

5

Cut a small square of paper to make a sail. Fold each end and glue or tape it to your mast, as shown.

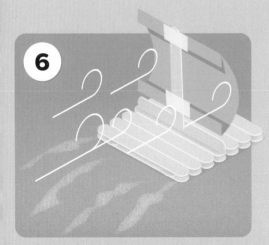

6

Test your raft in a bath, bowl, or sink. How well does it float? Try blowing on the sail. What happens now?

WHY IT WORKS

When you put the raft in water, two forces act upon it: the downward force of the raft's weight and the upward force of the water it moves. The large surface area of the raft means that the raft weighs less than (or the same as) the water it displaces. This makes it float. The sail is used to catch the wind to move the raft.

MAKE A PAPER POPPY

The travelers come across a great meadow of poppies. Try making your own colorful collection of poppies to brighten up your home.

YOU WILL NEED:

- thin red cardstock
- pencil
- scissors
- toothpick
- glue
- black paper
- printer size green cardstock

Using these templates as a guide, draw and cut out some 5-petal shapes and 3-petal shapes to form your flowers.

Roll the petals around the toothpick to give them a curled shape.

Put a spot of glue in the center of a 5-petal shape. Add a 5-petal shape on top at a different angle to alternate the petals.

4

Now add the 3-petal shapes to your flower in a similar manner.

5

Cut out a small circle of black paper and stick it in the middle of your flower. This is the flower's stamen.

6

Repeat to make as many poppies as you like. Stick them to the green cardstock to make a poppy meadow of your own.

WHY IT WORKS

Poppies are often grown for their colorful flowers. Some grow up to 3 feet (1 m) tall, with flowers up to 6 inches (15 cm) across. Poppies have often sprung up on deserted battlefields and are now regarded as a symbol of remembrance for fallen soldiers. One type of poppy is also used to make a powerful drug that can be used to treat pain and make you sleepy.

Chapter 5

Meeting the Wizard

The Lion was so grateful to be alive when he woke. They told him all about the mice before setting off to find the yellow-brick road. It was smooth and well-paved now with green-painted fences and green-painted houses. The people all wore green, too, with hats like the Munchkins. "We must be in the Land of Oz!" Dorothy said.

They stopped at the next house and Dorothy knocked boldly at the door. A woman answered. "What do you want child, and why is that Lion with you?"

"We're looking for somewhere to spend the night," Dorothy replied. "The Lion is my friend and won't hurt you."

"If that's the case, you may come in," the woman said.

They explained why they were going to the Emerald City. "I'm sure Oz can help you with all those things," the woman's husband remarked. "But the hardest task is to get to see him. I've been to the Emerald City many times. It's a beautiful place, but I don't know a living person who's seen Oz. He sits all day in the great Throne Room of his Palace, and even his servants don't see his face."

"What's he like?" Dorothy asked.

"Oz is a Great Wizard and can take on any form he wishes," the man said thoughtfully. "He appears as a fairy or a cat, or in any other form he likes. But who the real Oz is, no one knows."

"That's strange," said Dorothy, "but we must try to see him, or our journey will be in vain."

They set off next morning and saw a beautiful green glow far away. "That must be the Emerald City!" Dorothy exclaimed. Eventually, the road stopped at a big gate in the city walls. Dorothy pushed a bell and the gate opened to reveal a little man dressed in green. "What do you wish to find in the Emerald City?" he asked.

"We've come to see the Great Oz," Dorothy explained. The man was very surprised. "It's been many years since anyone's asked to see Oz," he said, shaking his head. "He's powerful and terrible, and he'll be angry if you've come on false pretences. I'm the Guardian of the Gates and I can take you to the Palace, but first you must put on these spectacles, so the brightness of the city doesn't blind you."

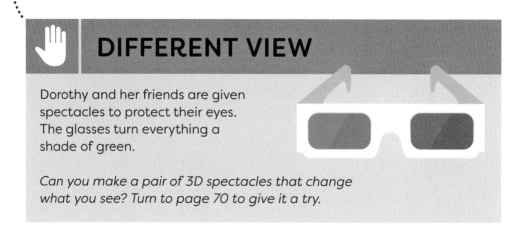

✋ DIFFERENT VIEW

Dorothy and her friends are given spectacles to protect their eyes. The glasses turn everything a shade of green.

Can you make a pair of 3D spectacles that change what you see? Turn to page 70 to give it a try.

LIGHT FILTERS

A light filter is a transparent material that absorbs some colors while allowing others to pass through. A green filter, for example, will let green light through but absorb other colors.

Light filters are used in many aspects of our lives. Traffic lights, for example, use light filters to tell us to stop (red) or go (green). Colored light bulbs can help to change the atmosphere of a room. Theater lights use filters for different moods and effects. In photography, light filters can be used to enhance some colors, or to minimize glare and reflections.

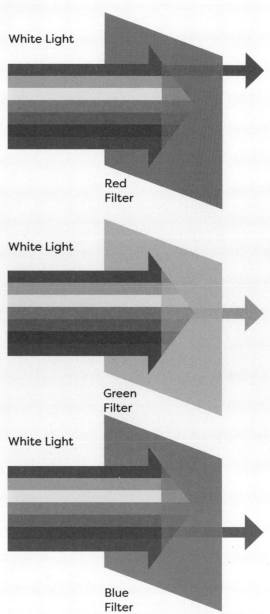

White Light

Red Filter

White Light

Green Filter

White Light

Blue Filter

The man opened a big box and found a pair of spectacles for Dorothy and locked them on with a little key. Then he fitted spectacles to the others, even Toto. Despite the spectacles, Dorothy and her friends were still dazzled by the wonderful city. The buildings were made from green marble and studded with sparkling emeralds. The windows were made from green glass, and even the sky had a green tint. All the people wore green clothes and had greenish skin. They looked quizzically at Dorothy and her friends, but no one spoke to them.

The Guardian of the Gates led them to the Palace. There was a soldier by the door with a long green beard and uniform. They were led into a big room with a green carpet and furniture. "Please make yourselves comfortable while I tell Oz you're here," the soldier said.

After a long time, he returned. "At first he said I should send you away. Then he asked what you looked like, and when I mentioned the silver shoes and the mark on your forehead, he decided to meet you. But each of you must enter alone, and only one each day. As you must remain here for several days, I'll show you to your rooms where you may rest." The soldier blew a green whistle, and a young girl took Dorothy to her room.

OPTICAL ILLUSIONS

Optical illusions are a trick of the mind. An optical illusion can make us see something that isn't really there or can change the way an image looks. Some optical illusions seem to be moving when they're actually still!

Optical illusions happen when our eyes send a signal to the brain that tricks us. Scientists think they work because our brains are so good at recognizing familiar objects in the world around us. Our brains work quickly to decipher what we see, but sometimes they get it wrong!

Take a look at some of the pictures below. What do you see? Do your friends see the same thing?

There was a comfortable bed with green silk sheets and a wardrobe full of green dresses. "Make yourself at home," the girl said, "and if you need anything, ring the bell. Oz will send for you tomorrow." She left Dorothy alone and took the others to their rooms, too.

The next morning, the girl dressed Dorothy in a pretty, green satin gown. The Throne Room was big and round with a high arched roof and the walls, ceiling, and floor were covered with large emeralds. In the center of the roof was a great light, as bright as the Sun, which made the emeralds sparkle. An enormous head, without a body, sat on a big throne of green marble in the middle of the room. It had a mouth, a nose, and eyes, but no hair.

As Dorothy gazed in wonder and fear, the eyes looked at her sharply. Then the mouth moved, "I am Oz, the Great and Terrible. Who are you, and why do you seek me?"

"I'm Dorothy, and I've come to you for help," she said courageously.

The eyes looked at her thoughtfully. "Where did you get the silver

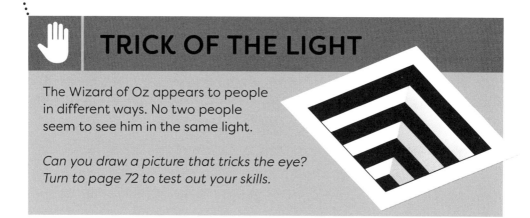

TRICK OF THE LIGHT

The Wizard of Oz appears to people in different ways. No two people seem to see him in the same light.

Can you draw a picture that tricks the eye? Turn to page 72 to test out your skills.

shoes and that mark upon
your forehead?"

"From the Wicked Witch of the
East, when my house fell on her
and killed her," Dorothy said.
"And the Good Witch of the
North kissed me when she sent
me to you."

Oz could see that she was telling
the truth. "What do you wish me
to do?" he asked.

"Send me back to Kansas," Dorothy said earnestly. "Your country is
beautiful, but Aunt Em will be worried, I've been away so long."

"Well," said the head. "If you want me to grant your wish, you must
kill the Wicked Witch of the West."

"But I can't!" exclaimed Dorothy with great surprise. "I've never killed
anything willingly," she sobbed. "Besides, you're great and if you can't
kill her yourself, how can *I* do it?"

"I don't know," the head replied, "but that's my answer, and until the
Wicked Witch dies, you won't see your aunt and uncle again. Don't
ask to see me until you've done your task."

Dorothy told her friends the terrible news, then ran back to her room
and cried herself to sleep.

The next morning, the Scarecrow was summoned. This time, he saw a lovely lady on the throne, dressed in silk and wearing a crown of jewels. She had wings that fluttered in the breeze. She looked at him sweetly and said, "I am Oz, the Great and Terrible. Who are you, and why do you seek me?"

"I am only a Scarecrow, stuffed with straw," he said bravely. "I'd love some brains like any other man."

"If you kill the Wicked Witch of the West, I'll give you a great many brains, so you'll be the wisest man in all the land," the lady continued.

"I thought you asked Dorothy to kill the Witch?" the Scarecrow said.

"I don't care who kills her, but until she's dead, I won't grant your wish. Now go."

The Scarecrow went sorrowfully back to his friends and told them what Oz had said.

The next morning, the Tin Man was summoned. He saw a terrible hairy beast sitting on the throne. It was nearly as big as an elephant, with a head like a rhinoceros, but with five eyes, five long arms, and five slim, long legs.

"I am Oz, the Great and Terrible," said the beast. "Who are you, and why do you seek me?"

"I'm a woodman made of tin," he replied. "I have no heart and cannot love. I beg you to give me a heart so I can be like other men."

"If you desire a heart, then you must earn it," Oz said gruffly. "Help Dorothy to kill the Wicked Witch of the West, and then I'll give you a loving heart."

The Tin Man returned sorrowfully to his friends to tell them what had happened.

The next morning, the Lion was summoned. He found a ball of fire before the throne, so fierce and glowing he could scarcely bear to gaze at it. A low, quiet voice came from the fire. "I am Oz, the Great and Terrible. Who are you, and why do you seek me?"

"I'm a cowardly Lion, afraid of everything," he answered. "I came to beg you to give me courage, so I may become the true King of the Beasts."

The ball of fire burned fiercely and then the voice said, "Bring me proof that the Wicked Witch is dead, and I'll give you courage. But as long as the Witch lives, you must remain a coward."

The Lion was angry but could say nothing in reply. He told his friends of the disappointing news.

MAKE YOUR OWN 3D GLASSES

Dorothy is given some green-tinted glasses so everything in the Emerald City looks green! Make some glasses of your own that alter what you see.

Using this template as a guide, cut out the basic shapes of your glasses.

YOU WILL NEED:

- white cardstock
- scissors • tape
- piece of clear plastic
- red and blue permanent markers

Use the red and blue markers to color rectangles on the piece of plastic. These will be your lenses.

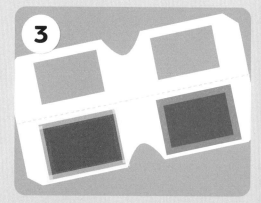

Cut the blue and red lenses out and tape them to the back of your glasses. Use the red lens for the left eye and the blue lens for the right eye.

4

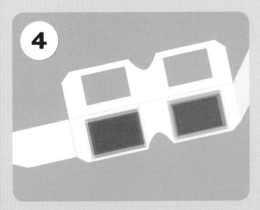

Now tape the arms onto your glasses.

5

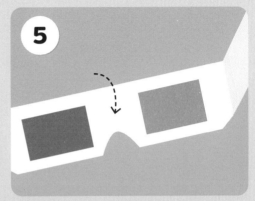

Finally, fold down the upper part of the glasses and tape to give your glasses more strength.

6

Now use your glasses to look at this 3D picture. What do you see?

WHY IT WORKS

3D glasses have red and blue lenses. When you look at a 3D picture, they filter out the layered image you're seeing. The red lens only lets red light through, while the blue lens only lets blue light through. This causes your brain to see the image as a three-dimensional shape. A 3D image is usually an image taken from two different angles, or two images on top of each other.

DRAW AN OPTICAL ILLUSION

The Wizard of Oz appears to Dorothy and her friends in different ways. Can you create an optical illusion that tests what you see? Try it out on your friends.

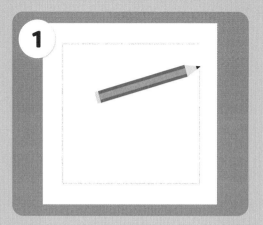

Draw a square on your piece of paper, as shown.

YOU WILL NEED:
- paper • pencil
- thin and thick black marker pens

Draw a diagonal line and then a border, as shown.

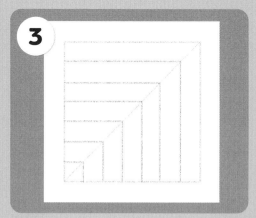

Continue adding these straight lines, as shown.

Draw over some of your lines with a thin marker and a thick marker, as shown.

Now color in alternate sections. Use your pencil to add shadows, as shown. Make the smallest section the darkest.

Look at your masterpiece. Do you see a flat piece of paper or a gaping hole? Show your picture to a friend—what do they see?

WHY IT WORKS

Shadows are caused when light is blocked by an object. If you add a cast shadow to a drawing, it gives the impression of a 3D shape. In this case, a cast shadow is used to give the impression of depth. The darkest shadow is found at the deepest part of the hole.

Chapter 6

Search for the Wicked Witch

"What shall we do now?" Dorothy asked sadly.

"There's only one thing we can do," said the Lion, "and that's go to the land of the Winkies, seek out the Wicked Witch, and destroy her."

"I suppose we must try it," said Dorothy, "or our wishes won't be granted. Although I don't want to kill anybody, even to see Aunt Em again." The others agreed to go with her the next morning.

When they awoke, the soldier took them to the Guardian of the Gates, who unlocked their spectacles and opened the gate for them.

"Which road leads to the Wicked Witch of the West?" Dorothy asked.

"There's no road," replied the Guardian of the Gates. "No one ever wishes to go that way."

"Then how are we to find her?" said Dorothy.

"That's easy," replied the man, "you need to go to the country of the Winkies. For when she knows you're there, she'll find you and try to make you all her slaves. Take care. If you wish to seek and destroy her, keep to the west, where the Sun sets, and you can't fail to find her."

NATURAL NAVIGATION

To find the Wicked Witch, Dorothy is told to keep to the west, where the Sun sets. She loses her way, however, because the Sun seems to travel across the sky.

The Sun rises in the east and sets in the west. It takes an average of 12 hours for the Sun to travel across the sky. You can use the Sun to find your way if you check and change your bearing every 10 minutes. Face the direction you want to travel and hold your arm out toward the Sun. Keep walking with the Sun in this position. Repeat every 10 minutes, so you keep your bearing in relation to the moving Sun. If the Sun is behind you, reach out your arm so it's in line with your shadow instead.

West

12 pm

2 pm

10 am

East

6 pm

6 am

They started walking westward over the fields of soft grass. Dorothy was still wearing the green silk dress from the Palace, but to her surprise, it had turned pure white, as had the ribbon around Toto's neck. Before long, the ground became rougher and hillier and there were no trees to offer shade from the Sun. Dorothy, Toto, and the Lion lay down to rest, while the Tin Man and Scarecrow kept watch.

The Wicked Witch of the West had just one eye, but it was as powerful as a telescope and could see everywhere. As she sat in the door of her yellow castle, she saw Dorothy lying asleep with her friends. The Witch was angry to find them in her country and blew a silver whistle that hung around her neck.

At once, a pack of wolves came running to her from all directions. "Go to those intruders," said the Witch, "and tear them to pieces."

"Are you not going to make them your slaves?" asked the wolf leader.

"No," replied the Witch, "one is of tin, one of straw, one is a girl, and another a lion. They are not fit to work and so you may tear them all to pieces."

ATTRACTING ATTENTION

The Wicked Witch of the West blows her silver whistle to call her servants. The high-pitched sound travels a long way.

Can you make a whistle to attract attention? Turn
to page 84 and see how loud you can make it sound.

Luckily, the Scarecrow and Tin Man were wide awake and heard the wolves coming. "This is my fight," said the Tin Man, "get behind me." He seized his axe and managed to kill the leader of the wolves as he approached, and then the 39 wolves that followed.

When Dorothy awoke the next morning, she was startled to see a pile of dead wolves, but the Tin Man explained what had happened. She thanked him for saving them and they set out on their journey.

Meanwhile, the Wicked Witch saw all her wolves lying dead, while the strangers were still alive. She was angrier than before, and she blew her silver whistle twice. A great flock of crows came flying toward her, enough to darken the sky.

"Fly at once to the strangers, peck out their eyes, and tear them to pieces," she said to the King Crow.

WHAT ARE THE CHANCES?

The Wicked Witch has 40 wolves and 40 crows to do her dirty deeds. Thankfully, the Tin Man and the Scarecrow manage to defeat them all.

Could you have predicted their chances? Turn to page 86 to test out some probability theories of your own.

SPEED OF SOUND

The Wicked Witch uses her whistle to attract the attention of her slaves, who come from far away.

Sounds travel when particles vibrate and bump into each other. Sounds don't travel in a vacuum for this reason because there are no particles for the vibrations to travel through.

In normal atmospheric conditions, the speed of sound is about 1,130 feet (344 m) per second— that's about 765 mph (1,230 kph)!

In water, sound travels about four times faster than it does in air! This is because the particles in water are closer together, so the sound vibrations travel through them more quickly.

Some animals, such as dogs and wolves, can hear particularly high-pitched sounds that humans cannot detect.

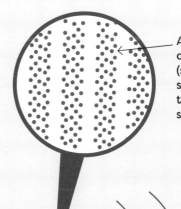

Air particles are compressed (squeezed) and stretched out to form the sound waves

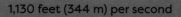

1,130 feet (344 m) per second

Dorothy was afraid of the crows, but the Scarecrow said, "This is my battle. Lie down beside me." The Scarecrow stretched out his arms and scared the birds away. But the King Crow said, "It's only a stuffed man. I will pcck his eyes out." He flew at the Scarecrow, who swatted him away and killed him, as well as the 39 crows that followed.

When the Wicked Witch saw all her crows lying in a heap, she got into a terrible rage, and blew her silver whistle three times. There was a buzzing sound, and a swarm of black bees came flying toward her. "Go to the strangers and sting them to death!" the Witch commanded.

When the Tin Man saw the bees coming, the Scarecrow knew what to do. "Take out my straw and scatter it over Dorothy, Toto, and the Lion," he said, "so the bees can't sting them." When the bees came, they could only find the Tin Man and their stings broke off, without hurting him at all. And without their stings, the bees died and lay scattered in a heap.

Dorothy and the Lion got up and helped the Tin Man to put the straw back into the Scarecrow again, before they restarted their journey.

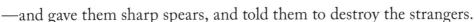

The Wicked Witch was so angry when she saw the heap of bees that she stamped her foot and tore at her hair. Then she called a dozen servants—the Winkies —and gave them sharp spears, and told them to destroy the strangers.

The Winkies weren't brave people, but they had to do as they were told. When they approached Dorothy and her friends, the Lion gave a great roar and sprang toward them, causing the Winkies to run away.

When the Winkies returned to the castle, the Wicked Witch beat them and sent them back to their work. She couldn't understand how all her plans had failed, but she soon decided what to do.

In her cupboard, the Witch had a charmed Golden Cap. Whoever owned the Cap could call three times upon the Winged Monkeys, who'd obey any order they were given. She had used the Cap twice already—once when she'd made the Winkies her slaves and once when she'd driven Oz away, so this was her final chance.

The Wicked Witch placed the Golden Cap on her head, stood upon her left foot and said slowly:
"Ep-pe, pep-pe, kak-ke!"

Then she stood on her right foot and said:
"Hil-lo, hol-lo, hel-lo!"

Then she stood on both feet and cried in a loud voice:
"Ziz-zy, zuz-zy, zik!"

The sky darkened and there was a rushing of many wings, a great chattering and laughing. When the Sun came out again, the Wicked Witch was surrounded by a crowd of monkeys, each with a pair of huge, powerful wings on his shoulders. "You've called us for the last time," the Monkey King said. "What do you command?"

"Go to the strangers in my land and destroy them all except the Lion," the Wicked Witch replied. "Bring that beast to me, for I want to harness him like a horse and make him work." Then with a great deal of chattering and noise, the Winged Monkeys flew off.

Some of the Monkeys seized the Tin Man and carried him through the air to a country covered with sharp rocks where they dropped him. The Tin Man fell a great distance, and he lay so battered and dented, he could neither move nor groan.

Other Monkeys caught the Scarecrow and pulled all the straw from his clothes and head before throwing a bundle of his clothes into the branches of a tall tree. The rest of the Monkeys threw a rope around the Lion and bound him tightly. They flew him to the Witch's castle, where he was imprisoned in a small yard with a high iron fence.

The Monkeys didn't harm Dorothy, however. As she stood with Toto in her arms, she watched the fate of her friends knowing it would be her turn next. But when the Monkey King saw the mark upon her forehead, he signaled to the others to leave her be.

"We daren't harm this girl," he said, "for she's protected by the Power of Good, which is greater than the Power of Evil. All we can do is carry her to the castle and leave her there."

The Monkeys carefully set Dorothy down on the doorstep of the castle. "We obeyed you as far as we could," the Monkey King explained to the Witch, "but we didn't dare harm the girl, nor the dog she carries. Your power over us has now ended, and you'll never see us again." And with that, all the Winged Monkeys flew out of sight.

The Wicked Witch was worried when she saw the mark on Dorothy's forehead, and the silver shoes made her tremble with fear. But when she looked into Dorothy's eyes, she saw the little girl didn't know the power she held. She laughed to herself and thought, "I can still make her my slave."

"Come with me," she said to Dorothy severely. "And do everything I tell you, for if you don't, I'll destroy you as I did the Tin Man and the Scarecrow."

MAKE A WHISTLE

The Wicked Witch of the West uses a silver whistle to summon her servants. Try making your own whistle to attract attention!

1

Cut a strip of thick aluminum,
1 x 4 inches (2.5 cm x 10 cm) in size.

YOU WILL NEED:

- sheet of thick aluminum
- scissors
- marker
- pencil

2

Wrap the metal around the marker pen, halfway along, to create a curved shape.

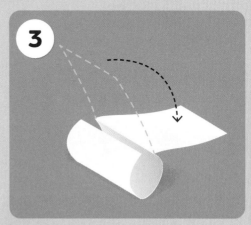

3

Bend the tip of your whistle slightly.

84

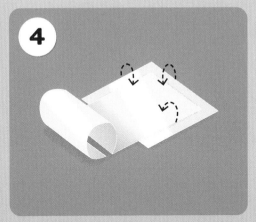

4 Take another small piece of aluminum, slightly larger than the whistle tip. Wrap it around the edges of the whistle tip.

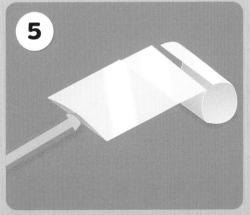

5 Use your pencil to make a small opening between the two sheets of aluminum.

6 Blow gently into your whistle to make a sound.

WHY IT WORKS

A whistle makes a high-pitched sound when air is forced through a small opening. The air rushes into the mouthpiece and escapes through the other side. Whistles are often used to attract attention—in sports matches, for example, or to call a dog back. Longer whistles produce a lower pitch and shorter whistles produce a higher pitch. Some whistles have a ball inside, which creates a warbling sound.

FINDING PROBABILITY

The Wicked Witch summons 40 wolves and 40 crows to attack the strangers in her land, but the Tin Man and Scarecrow manage to defeat them. Try this math challenge to see if you can overcome the odds!

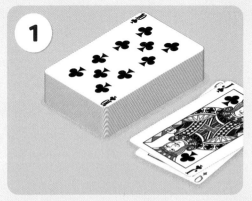

Remove the face cards (King, Queen, Jack) from the pack, leaving 40 cards remaining.

YOU WILL NEED:
- pack of cards
- pen or pencil
- notepad

Ask a friend to pick a card. What's the probability they'll pick a red card? Replace the card, shuffle and repeat five times.

Draw a tally chart, to show your prediction and the actual results.

4

Challenge	Prediction	Results out of 5

What's the probability they'll pick a multiple of 5 (if an Ace represents 1)? Replace, shuffle, and repeat as before.

5

What's the probability they'll pick a multiple of 2? What do you notice this time?

WHY IT WORKS

When you have 40 cards, the theoretical probability of picking a red card is 20/40 (or 1/2). This is because half the cards are red. The probability of picking a multiple of 5 is 8/40 (or 1/5) because you have a 5 and a 10 in each of the four suits. The probability of picking a multiple of 2 is 20/40 (or 1/2) because you have 2, 4, 6, 8 and 10 in each of the four suits. You'll notice that the probability of picking a red card equals the probability of picking a multiple of 2. The more times you repeat the experiment, the closer you'll get to the theoretical probability.

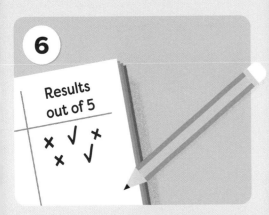

6

Results out of 5
✗ ✓ ✗
✗ ✓

Look at your results. How close were your predicted probabilities to the actual results? What would happen if you repeated the task more times?

Chapter 7

The Rescue

The Witch took Dorothy to the kitchen, where she made her clean and sweep, and tend the fire. Dorothy worked very hard because she was glad her life had been spared.

The Witch went to harness the Lion, but he gave a great roar and bounded at her so fiercely, she became afraid. "If I can't harness you, I'll starve you," she said. But her plan was in vain. Every night Dorothy secretly took food to the Lion, and they'd lie together on his bed of straw and talk of how they might escape.

The Witch didn't dare strike Dorothy because of the mark on her forehead. Dorothy didn't know this of course, so she was full of fear. The Wicked Witch was desperate to have Dorothy's silver shoes. Her bees, crows, and wolves had died, and she'd used the power of the Golden Cap. If she could just get hold of the silver shoes, they'd give her more power than ever. But Dorothy only took them off at night and when she had a bath. The Witch was too afraid of the dark to steal them at night, and she dreaded water. In fact, the Witch never let any water touch her.

But the Witch had a cunning plan. She put an iron bar on the kitchen floor and made it invisible. When Dorothy stumbled over the bar, she lost one of her silver shoes, and the Witch quickly snatched it away.

The Witch was delighted—with one shoe, she owned half the power of their charm, and Dorothy couldn't use it against her. "You're wicked!" Dorothy cried. "You've no right to take my shoe." She was so angry, she picked up a bucket of water and threw it over the Witch, wetting her from head to toe.

Immediately, the woman gave a loud cry of fear, and then, as Dorothy looked at her in wonder, the Witch began to shrink and fall away.

"See what you've done!" the Witch said in a wailing voice. "In a few minutes I'll be melted, and you'll have the castle to yourself. I've been wicked, but I never thought a girl like you would be my end!"

With these words, the Witch fell down in a shapeless mass. Once she had melted away to nothing, Dorothy threw another bucket of water over the mess and swept it away. She cleaned and dried the silver shoe before placing it back on her foot. Then, she ran to tell the Lion they  were free and the Winkies were delighted they were no longer slaves.

 # SPINNING AROUND

Dorothy throws a bucket of water over the Wicked Witch. The force of gravity pulls the water down to cover the Witch from head to toe.

Can you swing a bucket of water without getting wet? *Turn to page 98 to find out how.*

MELTING POINTS

Water makes the Wicked Witch shrink and melt away. The melting point of a substance is the temperature at which it changes from a solid to a liquid. Different materials have different melting points.

Scientists have worked out the melting points of substances. The melting point of pure water, for example, is 32°F (0°C), while the melting point of chocolate is about 122°F (50°C) and candle wax about 158°F (70°C).

Melting points are useful in many everyday applications. Metals and plastics, for example, can be melted and molded into different shapes, before they cool and become a solid again.

Melting can also separate substances with different melting points. For example, iron can be separated from iron ore (a mixture of iron and minerals) by heating it to 2,800°F (1,538°C) so the iron melts into a collecting chamber.

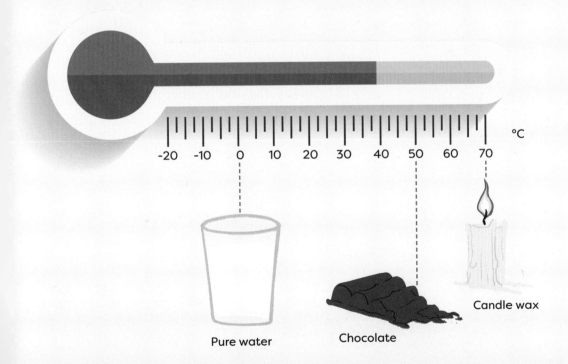

°C

-20 -10 0 10 20 30 40 50 60 70

Pure water   Chocolate   Candle wax

"If only the Scarecrow and Tin Man were with us," said the Lion. "I would be quite happy."

They called the Winkies together, who said they'd be delighted to help rescue their friends. They came to the rocky plain where the Tin Man lay battered and bent. His axe was nearby but the blade was rusted, and the handle had split.

The Winkies carefully carried the Tin Man back to the castle. Some of them were tinsmiths who set to work hammering and soldering until he was as good as new. They repaired his axe, too.

"If only we had the Scarecrow with us," said the Tin Man, when Dorothy told him everything that had happened. "I should be quite happy."

Dorothy called the Winkies to help once more. They came to the tall tree with the Scarecrow's clothes in its branches. It was difficult to climb but the Tin Man chopped it down. The Winkies carried the clothes back to the castle, where they were stuffed with clean straw, and behold! There was the Scarecrow, as good as new, thanking them for saving him.

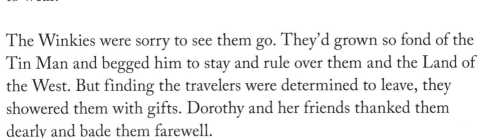

They spent a few happy days reunited before setting out for the Emerald City again. Dorothy went to fill her basket from the Witch's cupboard, and came across the Golden Cap, which fitted her well. She didn't know about its charm, but thought it was pretty to wear.

The Winkies were sorry to see them go. They'd grown so fond of the Tin Man and begged him to stay and rule over them and the Land of the West. But finding the travelers were determined to leave, they showered them with gifts. Dorothy and her friends thanked them dearly and bade them farewell.

There was no road between the castle and the Emerald City, so it was harder to find their way. They knew they must go east, toward the rising Sun, but at noon, when the Sun was overhead, they didn't know which was east or west, and were soon lost in the great fields.

Days passed and they still saw nothing but scarlet fields. "Unless we reach the Emerald City," the Scarecrow complained, "I shall never get my brains." They all felt exasperated.

"Perhaps we should call the field mice?" Dorothy suggested. She blew a little whistle around her neck the Queen had given her, and within minutes, they heard a pattering of tiny feet running toward them. "What can I do for you, my friends?" the Queen of the Mice asked.

MIGRATION

Dorothy and her friends travel east toward the rising Sun. Every year, many species of birds migrate thousands of miles to find favorable weather and plentiful food. Many species find their way back to the same feeding or breeding grounds.

Scientists don't know exactly how birds manage to navigate their way. While some birds may recognize landmarks, other theories suggest birds use the position of the Sun or the stars. Researchers have also found special cells in birds' eyes that may help them to "see" Earth's magnetic field, and a small spot of magnetic magnetite on the beaks of some birds—perhaps giving them a built-in GPS system!

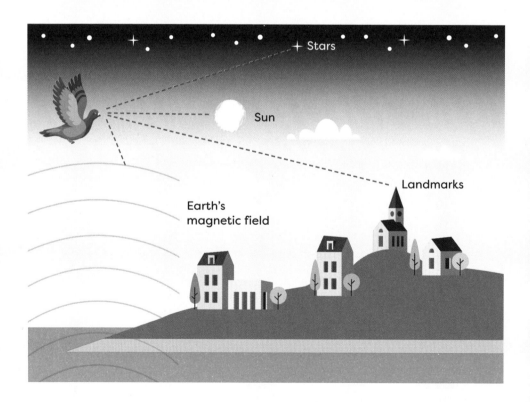

+ Stars

Sun

Landmarks

Earth's magnetic field

"Can you tell us the way to the Emerald City?" said Dorothy.

"Certainly," said the Queen, "it's been behind you all this time." Then she noticed the Golden Cap. "Why don't you use the Cap and call the Winged Monkeys? They'll carry you to the Emerald City."

"I didn't know it could do that," said Dorothy in surprise.

"The charm is written inside the Cap," the Queen explained. "But if you call the Winged Monkeys, we must go. Goodbye!" and she scampered out of sight, with all the mice hurrying after her.

Dorothy looked at the Cap and recited the words written in the lining.

"Ep-pe, pep-pe, kak-ke!" she said, standing on her left foot.

"Hil-lo, hol-lo, hel-lo!" she added, standing on her right foot.

"Ziz-zy, zuz-zy, zik!" she exclaimed, standing on both feet. At once, they heard a great chattering and flapping of wings, as the band of Winged Monkeys flew up to them.

✋ HATS OFF!

Dorothy comes across the Golden Cap in the Witch's cupboard. It's pretty and a perfect fit, but it also has a powerful charm!

Can you make a Golden Cap of your own with just a piece of paper?
Turn to page 100 for some tips.

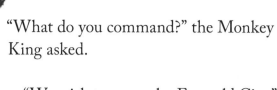

"What do you command?" the Monkey King asked.

"We wish to go to the Emerald City," said Dorothy.

No sooner had she spoken, the Monkeys gathered them in their arms and were flying away.

The Scarecrow and Tin Man were rather frightened at first, for they remembered how badly the Winged Monkeys had treated them before, but they soon saw no harm was intended. Dorothy was riding between two of the biggest Monkeys, one of them the King himself.

"Why do you have to obey the charm of the Golden Cap?" she asked.

"That's a long story," answered the King, with a laugh, "but as we have a long journey before us, I'll tell you."

"Many years ago, before Oz came to rule over this land," the King began, "we were a free people, living happily in the great forest. A beautiful princess and powerful sorceress called Gayelette lived in the North. Everyone loved her, but she couldn't find anyone to love in return. All the men were too stupid or ugly to be with someone so beautiful and wise. At last, however, she found a handsome boy named Quelala who was wise beyond his years. Gayelette decided she'd marry him when he grew to be a man. At that time, my grandfather was the Monkey King who lived by Gayelette's palace. Just before the wedding, he and his band saw Quelala walking beside the river. For a joke, they picked him up and dropped him into the water.

"Quelala laughed and swam back to the shore. But when Gayelette found his silk and velvet clothes were ruined, she was angry. She wanted to drown the Monkeys in the river, but Quelala said to spare them. Instead, she said they must follow three orders of the owner of the Golden Cap, which had been made as a wedding present to Quelala."

"And what became of them?" asked Dorothy.

"Quelala was the first owner of the Cap," replied the Monkey King. "He ordered us to stay away from his wife. But then the Cap fell into the hands of the Wicked Witch of the West, who made us enslave the Winkies, and drive Oz away."

As the King finished his story, Dorothy could see the green, shining walls of the Emerald City. She was amazed at the speed of the flight but was glad the journey was over. The Monkeys set the travelers down carefully by the city gate, before flying swiftly away.

"That was a good ride," said Dorothy.

"Yes, and a quick way out of our troubles," replied the Lion. "How lucky it was you brought away that wonderful Cap!"

CREATE A CENTRIPETAL FORCE

Dorothy throws a bucket of water over the Wicked Witch. If she'd swung the bucket around and around, the water wouldn't have splashed so much! Find out how, with this simple experiment.

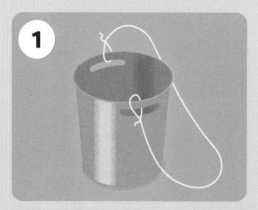

1

Tie the rope to the bucket, to create a looped handle.

YOU WILL NEED:

• bucket with two handles
• piece of rope 3 feet (1 m) long
• water

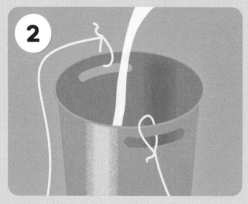

2

Fill the bucket with enough water so that it's not too heavy to lift.

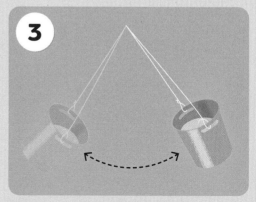

3

Stand in an open space outside and swing your bucket from side to side to get used to the motion.

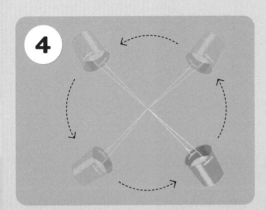

When you're ready, swing the bucket around quite quickly in a full circle.

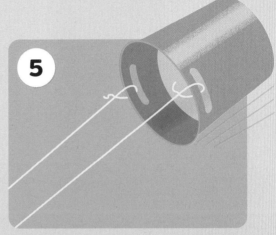

Repeat this action a few times. What do you notice about the water?

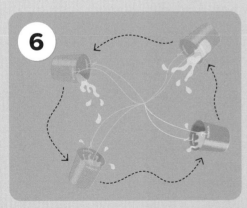

What do you think will happen if you move the bucket more slowly?

WHY IT WORKS

Objects move in a straight line at a constant speed unless a force acts upon them. This is called inertia. The rope handle pulls on the bucket to change its direction of motion. This "centripetal force" causes the bucket to move in a circle. If you let go of the bucket, it would fly off in a straight line. When the bucket is upside down, gravity wants to pull the water down, but the centripetal force is stronger. If you slow down your movement, the pull of gravity becomes stronger than the centripetal force and you get wet!

MAKE A GOLDEN CAP

Dorothy comes across the Golden Cap in the Witch's cupboard but doesn't realize the power of its charm. Try creating a Golden Cap of your own, and make a wish!

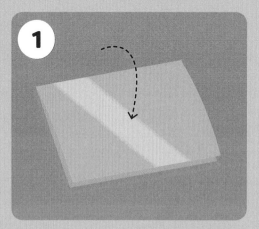

1

Fold the gold paper in half lengthways, as shown.

YOU WILL NEED:

- 2 sheets of printer-size gold paper
- foil stickers

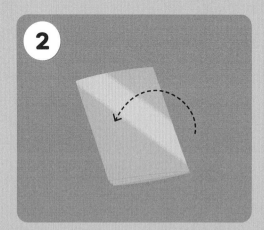

2

Fold the paper in half again, widthways.

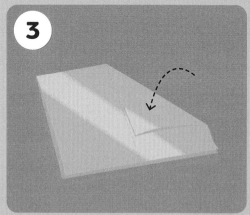

3

Open your last fold, and fold the right corner down diagonally, as shown.

4

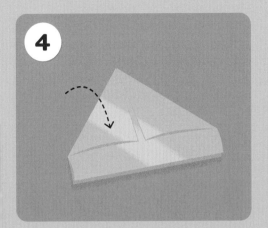

Repeat with the left corner.

5

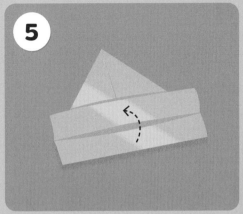

Now fold the bottom flap upward. Repeat on the other side.

6

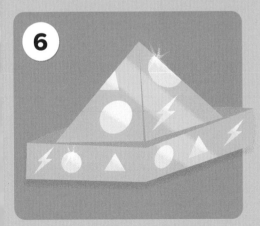

Decorate your Golden Cap with foil stickers. You could use the other piece of paper to try a different design! What would *you* wish for?

WHY IT WORKS

Origami is the ancient art of paper folding. While a thin piece of paper is floppy and weak, creating folds gives it strength. Tucks and folds also keep the paper together, without the need for glue, staples, or tape. Folding the paper in half, and repeating folds on each side, also gives your design some symmetry. No one wants a crooked hat!

Chapter 8

Discovering Oz the Great

"You're back again?" the Guardian of the Gates said in surprise.
"Did the Wicked Witch let you go?"

"She had to," the Scarecrow cried. "Dorothy melted her!"

"Good gracious!" exclaimed the man, and he bowed very low before
Dorothy. When the people of the Emerald City heard what Dorothy
had done, they all gathered around and followed them in a great
crowd to the Palace.

The soldier let them in at once, and the green girl showed them to
their rooms so they could rest until Oz was ready to receive them.

They thought Oz would send for them at once, but there was no word
from him the next day, or the next, or the one after that. Eventually,
the Scarecrow asked the green girl to tell Oz if he didn't see them at
once, they'd call the Winged Monkeys. Oz was so frightened, he sent
for them the next morning. He didn't wish to meet the Winged
Monkeys again.

The four travelers couldn't sleep that night, each thinking of the gift
Oz had promised them. They were greatly surprised when there was
no one in the Throne Room this time.

Then a solemn voice seemed to come from the top of the great dome. "I am Oz, the Great and Terrible. Why do you seek me?"

"Where are you?" Dorothy asked.

"I'm everywhere," answered the voice, "but to the eyes of common mortals, I'm invisible. I'll seat myself upon my throne, so you can speak with me." And the voice indeed seemed to move.

"You promised to send me back to Kansas when the Wicked Witch was destroyed," Dorothy began. "I melted her with a bucket of water."

"Goodness, how sudden!" the voice replied. "Well, come to me tomorrow, for I need time to think it over."

"You've had plenty of time already," said the Tin Man angrily, and the Lion gave a great roar. The sound was so fierce, Toto jumped in alarm and tipped over the screen in the corner. As it fell with a crash, they were astounded to see a little old man, with a bald head and a wrinkled face, who seemed to be just as surprised as they were.

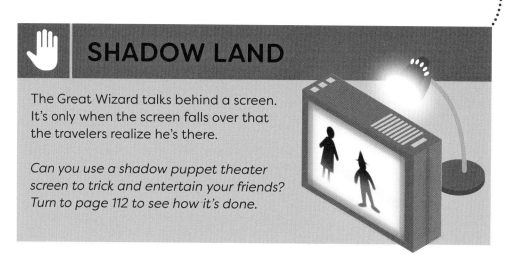

SHADOW LAND

The Great Wizard talks behind a screen. It's only when the screen falls over that the travelers realize he's there.

Can you use a shadow puppet theater screen to trick and entertain your friends? *Turn to page 112 to see how it's done.*

"Who are you?" the Tin Man cried, raising his axe.

"I am Oz, the Great and Terrible," the little man replied, in a trembling voice. "But don't strike me, please. I'll do anything you want."

The four friends looked at him in dismay. "Are you not a Great Wizard?" Dorothy cried.

"Don't speak so loud or you'll be overhead," Oz pleaded. "I'm supposed to be a Great Wizard, but I'm just a common man."

"This is terrible," said the Tin Man. "How shall I ever get my heart?"

"I pray you not to speak of these little things," said Oz. "Think of the terrible trouble I'm in at being found out. I've fooled everyone for so long. It was a great mistake to let you into the Throne Room."

"I don't understand," said Dorothy. "How did you appear to me as a great head?"

"Come this way and I'll show you." He led them to a small chamber in the rear of the Throne Room and pointed to a great head made from papier-mâché, with a carefully painted face. "I hung this from the ceiling," Oz said. "I stood behind the screen and pulled a thread to make it move. I'm a ventriloquist so I can throw the sound of my voice."

VENTRILOQUIZING

The Wizard has learned the art of ventriloquizing to "throw" the sound of his voice. He can't actually make his voice come from a different direction, but he tricks Dorothy and her friends into believing this is so.

Ventriloquists talk without moving their mouth. They often have a puppet (or "dummy") that moves its mouth, so it looks like the puppet is talking. When sound enters our ears, signals are sent to our brain. When these are combined with "visual" clues, our brains can be confused. We associate the moving mouth with sound, so we think the sound is coming from that direction.

Hello!

IN A SPIN

The Wizard's hot air balloon needed warm air to rise, but it also needed cool air to come down again. We call these air movements "convection currents."

Turn to page 114 to make a spinning snake that shows convection currents in action.

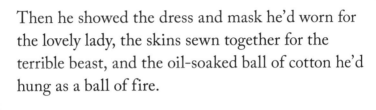

Then he showed the dress and mask he'd worn for the lovely lady, the skins sewn together for the terrible beast, and the oil-soaked ball of cotton he'd hung as a ball of fire.

"You ought to be ashamed of yourself," said the Scarecrow.

"I am," answered the man sorrowfully, "but I had no choice. Let me tell you my story."

"I was born in Omaha and when I grew up, I became a ventriloquist. But after a time, I tired of that and became a balloonist to draw a crowd on circus day. One day the balloon ropes got twisted and I couldn't get down. The balloon went so high that a current of air carried it many miles away. For a day and a night, I traveled through the air, and on the second morning, the balloon floated down over a strange and beautiful country.

AIR CURRENTS

When the Sun heats the Earth's surface, it warms some areas more than others. The Equator is warmed more than the Poles, for example.

When air above the Earth's surface is warmed, it rises, while cold air rushes down to replace it. This is because warm air is less dense than cold air—its molecules move faster and farther apart. This rising and falling air causes areas of high and low pressure. As warm air rises, it causes low pressure at the surface, but as cooler air falls, it causes high pressure at the surface. We call these air movements "convection currents." You sometimes see birds gliding on currents of air, and it was these currents that carried the Wizard's hot air balloon away.

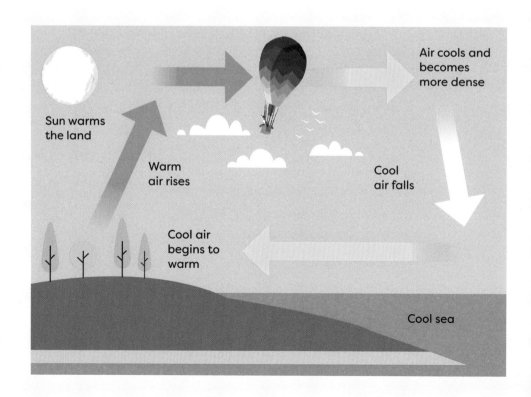

Sun warms the land

Warm air rises

Cool air begins to warm

Air cools and becomes more dense

Cool air falls

Cool sea

"Seeing me come down from the clouds, the people thought I was a great Wizard and they promised to do anything I wished. Just to amuse myself, I ordered them to build this city and my Palace.

"I called it Emerald City and used green spectacles so everything they saw was green. My people have worn the glasses for so long, they think it really is an Emerald City.

"My greatest fear was the Wicked Witches. Luckily, they thought I was more powerful than them, or they'd have surely destroyed me. You can imagine how pleased I was when the Wicked Witch of the East was killed. I was willing to promise anything if you'd kill the Wicked Witch of the West. But now you've melted her, I'm ashamed to say I can't keep my promises."

"I think you're a very bad man," said Dorothy.

"Can't you give me brains?" asked the Scarecrow.

"You don't need them," said the Wizard. "You're learning something every day. Experience is the only thing that brings knowledge. But if you come tomorrow, I'll stuff your head with brains. I can't tell you how to use them though, you'll have to figure that out yourself."

"But what about my courage?" asked the Lion anxiously.

"You have plenty of courage," answered Oz. "All you need is confidence in yourself. True courage is facing danger even when you're afraid, and you have plenty of that. But I can give you some more courage tomorrow."

"What about my heart?" asked the Tin Man.

"I think you're wrong to want a heart," Oz replied. "It makes most people unhappy, but if you want to come tomorrow, I'll give you a heart."

"And how will I get back to Kansas?" Dorothy asked.

"Give me two or three days to work that out," he said. "In the meantime, you're welcome as my guests, as long as you keep my secret." Dorothy was full of hope that Oz would help her back to Kansas, and if he did, she was willing to forgive him.

The next morning, the Scarecrow went to see Oz to get some brains. "You must excuse me for taking your head off," said Oz, "but it's necessary to put your brains in their proper place." He emptied out the straw and got a measure of bran which he mixed with a great many pins and needles. He filled the top of the Scarecrow's head with the mixture before securing it back on.

"There, you'll be a great man now," he said, "I've given you a lot of bran-new brains." The Scarecrow thanked him warmly and returned to his friends.

Then the Tin Man went to get his heart. "I shall have to cut a hole in your chest," Oz said, "so I can put your heart in the right place. I hope it won't hurt you."

"Oh, I won't feel it at all," said the Tin Man. Oz used some tinsmith's shears to cut a small hole, and took a pretty heart from the cupboard, made of silk and stuffed with sawdust. He put it in the Tin Man's chest and soldered the hole together again. "Now you have a heart any man might be proud of." The Tin Man was very grateful.

Then the Lion went to get his courage. Reaching up to a high shelf, Oz got a square green bottle and poured its contents into a green-gold dish. He placed it before the Lion and told him to drink.

"What is it?" asked the Lion. "If it were inside you, it would be courage," Oz answered. "So I advise that you drink it as soon as possible." The Lion drank the dish until it was empty.

"How do you feel?' asked Oz.

"Full of courage," replied the Lion, who went joyfully back to his friends.

Oz smiled to himself, thinking how he'd given them what they'd wanted. "How can I help being a humbug," he said, "when all these people make me do things everybody knows are impossible? It was easy to make them happy because they imagined I could do anything. But it will take more than imagination to carry Dorothy back to Kansas, and I don't know how it can be done."

CREATE A SHADOW PUPPET THEATER

The Great Oz's voice comes from behind a screen, so he can trick the travelers. Create a shadow puppet theater screen to trick and entertain your friends.

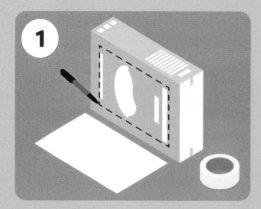

YOU WILL NEED:

- empty cereal box
- pencil and ruler
- scissors
- tape
- sheet of printer paper
- black cardstock
- wooden craft sticks or skewers
- metal brads
- small lamp

Tape the cereal box lids down to keep the box sturdy. Hold the paper on one side of the box. Mark a border on the box about 1 inch (2.5 cm) inside the paper.

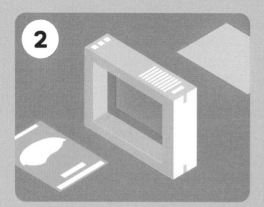

Ask an adult to help you cut out this rectangle with a craft knife and repeat on the other side.

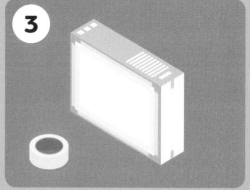

Tape the paper over one of the rectangle holes. This will be the front of your theater.

4

Using the black cardstock, draw characters for your show and cut them out.

5

Tape a wooden craft stick or skewer to the back of each character. You can also create moving parts with the metal brads. Tape a stick to each part so you can move them.

6

Set your theater up in a dark room. Place a lamp behind the theater and move your characters behind the screen, to give your audience a show!

WHY IT WORKS

Shadow puppets have been used for thousands of years as a form of entertainment. When you place your puppet between a lamp and the screen, the puppet blocks the light rays and casts a shadow on the screen. You can make your puppets move—and speak for them—to create a realistic shadow performance.

MAKE A SPINNING SNAKE

Warm air caused the Wizard's hot air balloon to rise. The balloon didn't fall until the air cooled again. Make your own spinning snake to see how warm air creates movement in other ways.

1

Using this template as a guide, draw a spiral for your snake.

YOU WILL NEED:

- printer paper
- pencil
- marker pens
- scissors
- string
- radiator (or bowl of hot water)

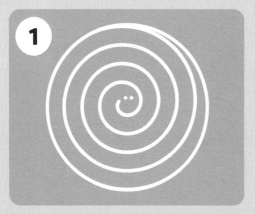

2

Use the marker to color in your snake with whatever decoration you choose.

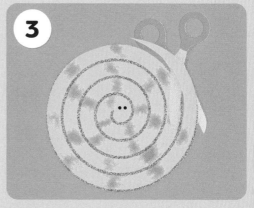

3

Now cut around the lines.

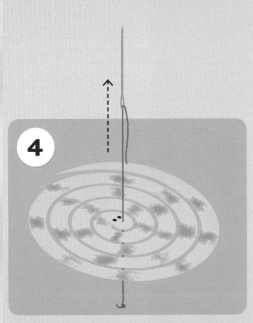

4

Ask an adult to help you thread a piece of string through the snake's head. Tie with a small knot to secure.

5

Hold the snake by the string. What do you notice?

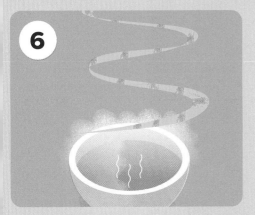

6

Now hold your snake above a warm radiator or a bowl of hot water. What do you notice this time?

WHY IT WORKS

When air is heated, its molecules move faster and farther apart. This causes warm air to rise. In contrast, cool air falls because the molecules slow down and move closer together. A heat source, such as a radiator or bowl of hot water, warms the air above it. As the warm air rises, it causes the snake to rotate. At the same time, cool air falls and pushes down on the snake, causing it to spin as well. We call these air movements "convection currents."

Chapter 9

Journey to the Desert

For three days, Dorothy heard nothing from Oz. Although her friends were quite content, her heart was full of sorrow as she longed to get back to Kansas. On the fourth day, to her great joy, Oz sent for her.

"Sit down, my dear. I think I've found a way to get you home. I came here in a balloon, and you were carried through the air by a tornado. I believe I can make a silk balloon coated in glue to take you across the desert. We can use hot air to make it rise, as long as it doesn't get cold and bring us down in the desert or we'll be lost."

"We!" exclaimed Dorothy. "Are you going with me?"

"Yes, of course," replied Oz. "I'm tired of being such a humbug. I stay shut up in my Palace in case people discover I'm not a Wizard but I'd much rather go back to Kansas with you and be in a circus again."

It took three days to sew the balloon, but when it was finished they had a big bag of green silk more than 20 feet (6 m) long. Oz painted the inside with glue to make it airtight, and fastened a large clothes basket to the bottom.

Oz put out word that he was going to visit a great brother wizard who lived in the clouds. The news spread rapidly, and everyone came to see the wonderful sight as the balloon was launched in front of the Palace.

The Tin Man chopped a big pile of wood to make a fire, and the hot air was caught in the silken bag. Gradually, the balloon swelled and rose into the air, until finally the basket began to lift from the ground.

As Oz got into the basket he said in a loud voice, "While I'm gone, the Scarecrow will rule over you. I command you to obey him." By now, the balloon was tugging at the rope that held it down. "Come, Dorothy!" cried the Wizard. "Hurry, or the balloon will fly away."

"I can't find Toto," Dorothy replied. Toto had run into the crowd. Dorothy found him at last and picked him up, when, suddenly the ropes snapped, and the balloon rose into the air without her.

"Come back!" she screamed. "I want to go, too!"

"I can't come back, my dear," Oz called from the basket. "Goodbye!"

"Goodbye!" shouted everyone, as they watched the Wizard rising farther into the sky. That was the last anyone saw of Oz. The people grieved for many days and remembered him lovingly.

UP AND AWAY

Dorothy and the Wizard make a hot air balloon by sewing silk together and coating it with glue. It takes them three days to create it.

Can you make a simple hot air balloon from a shopping bag? Turn to page 126 to see how it can be done.

AIR DENSITY

The density of air changes as it warms and cools. When air is heated, the molecules move faster and farther apart. This creates less dense air. When air is cooled, the molecules move more slowly and come closer together. This creates denser air.

Warm air rises because it is lighter than the cooler air that surrounds it. Air density is also affected by pressure. When you pump up your bicycle tires, you force more air into the tire tube, which increases the air density there. Air pressure decreases the higher you go from the Earth's surface. Mountaineers carry oxygen cylinders, for example, because the air on a mountaintop is less dense, so there is less oxygen found there.

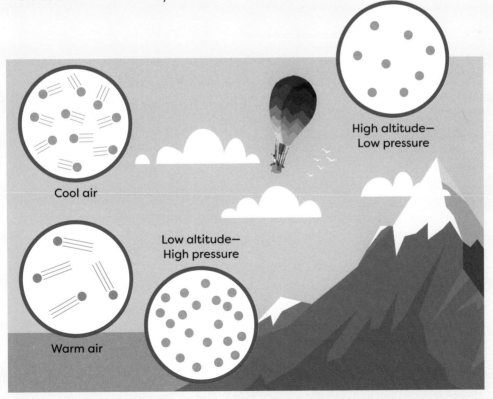

Cool air

High altitude—
Low pressure

Low altitude—
High pressure

Warm air

Dorothy wept bitterly as her hopes of reaching Kansas were dashed, and she grieved for the loss of the Wizard, too. The Scarecrow was now the ruler of the Emerald City, and the people were proud of him.

The next morning, the four travelers met in the Throne Room. "If Dorothy would only be content to live in the Emerald City, we might all be happy together."

"But I don't want to live here," cried Dorothy. "I want to live with Aunt Em and Uncle Henry."

"Why not call the Winged Monkeys and ask them to carry you over the desert?" the Scarecrow suggested.

"I never thought of that!" said Dorothy joyfully. She went to get the Golden Cap and as soon as she'd spoken the magic words, the band of Winged Monkeys flew through the open window and stood beside her.

"What do you command?" said the Monkey King.

"I want you to fly with me to Kansas," explained Dorothy. But the Monkey King shook his head.

"That can't be done," he said. "We belong to this country only and we cannot leave it. Goodbye." The Monkeys spread their wings and flew away.

"I've wasted the charm for nothing!" Dorothy exclaimed.

"Let us ask the soldier's advice," the Scarecrow suggested, and they explained their predicament.

"Nobody's ever crossed the desert," the soldier said, "but Glinda might be able to help you, the Good Witch of the South. She's the most powerful of all the Witches, and rules over the Quadlings. Besides, her castle stands on the edge of the desert, so she may know a way to cross it."

"How can I get to her castle?" Dorothy asked.

"The road is straight to the south," he answered, "but it's said to be full of dangers. For this reason, none of the Quadlings ever come to the Emerald City." And with that the soldier left.

"It seems Dorothy must travel to ask Glinda for help," the Scarecrow said. "If she stays here, she'll never get back to Kansas." They all agreed to go with her the next morning.

As they bid farewell to the Guardian of the Gates, he said to the Scarecrow, "You're now our ruler, so come back to us as soon as possible."

"I certainly shall," the Scarecrow replied, "but I must help Dorothy get home first."

The Sun shone brightly as the travelers turned their faces toward the south. "City life doesn't agree with me at all," remarked the Lion. "I've lost much flesh since I lived there, and now I want to show the other beasts how courageous I've grown."

"Oz was not such a bad Wizard, after all," said the Tin Man, as he felt his heart rattling around in his chest. "He knew how to give me brains, and very good brains, too," added the Scarecrow. "If Oz had taken a dose of the same courage that he gave me," said the Lion, "he'd have been a brave man." Dorothy said nothing. Oz had not kept the promise he'd made, but he'd done his best, so she forgave him.

They traveled through fields of bright flowers that stretched around the Emerald City on every side and slept that night on the grass. The next morning, they came to a thick wood. There was no way to go around it, so they looked for a way in.

The Scarecrow found a big tree with such wide-spreading branches, there was room for the party to pass underneath. But just as he went forward, the branches bent down and twined around him, lifting him up and flinging him back again. The Scarecrow wasn't hurt, but when Dorothy picked him up, he felt rather dizzy and surprised.

"Here's another space between the trees," called the Lion.

"Let me try first," said the Scarecrow, "I don't get hurt if I'm thrown about." But the branches immediately seized him and tossed him back again.

"What shall we do?" exclaimed Dorothy.

"I believe I should try," said the Tin Man, shouldering his axe. He marched up to the first tree and when a big branch tried to seize him, he chopped at it so fiercely, he cut it in two.

At once, the tree began shaking all its branches as if in pain, and the Tin Man passed through safely.

"Come on!" he shouted to the others. "Be quick!" They all ran underneath. Thankfully, the other trees didn't hold them back. They walked with ease until they came to the far edge of the wood where to their surprise, they found a high wall made of white china. It was smooth, like the surface of a dish, and higher than their heads.

"What shall we do now?" asked Dorothy.

"I'll make a ladder," said the Tin Man.

CHINA CLAY

Kaolin (china clay) is a soft white clay mineral found in the ground. It was discovered and used in China over 10,000 years ago to make white porcelain and is named after Kaoling—a hill in China where it was first found and mined.

When kaolin is mixed with water, it can be molded into different shapes. When it is dried (using heat), the water evaporates from the clay and it changes from a soft, malleable material to become rock-hard.

Its whiteness and fine, soft particles make it a particularly good material for tableware. However, china clay is also used to make other products, such as glossy paper, cement, bricks, paint, and toothpaste!

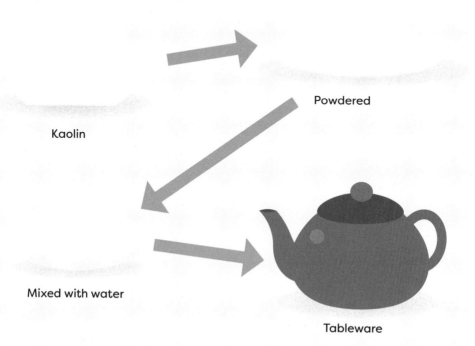

Kaolin

Powdered

Mixed with water

Tableware

MAKING SHAPES

It must be strange to come across a country made entirely of china, where everything's been made or molded in some way.

Try your hand at making a clay pot.
Turn to page 128 for some useful tips.

The Scarecrow climbed the ladder first, with Dorothy behind him, and when he got to the top of the wall he exclaimed, "Oh, my!" Dorothy came up next. "Oh, my!" she cried, just as the Scarecrow had done. When they were all sitting in a row on top of the wall, they looked down and saw a strange sight.

Before them was a great stretch of country, with a smooth white floor. Scattered around were many houses made entirely of china and painted in the brightest colors. The biggest reached only as high as Dorothy's waist. There were also pretty barns, with fences and farm animals, all made of china. But the strangest of all were the china people, no taller than Dorothy's knee.

"How shall we get down?" Dorothy asked.

The ladder was too heavy to pull up, so the Scarecrow fell off the wall and the others jumped on top of him to cushion their fall. When they were all down, they patted the Scarecrow's straw into shape again.

"We must cross this strange land," said Dorothy, "for it would be unwise for us to go any other way except due south."

MAKE A HOT-AIR BALLOON

It takes three days for Dorothy and the Wizard to make their hot-air balloon. See if you can create a balloon of your own, and make it rise!

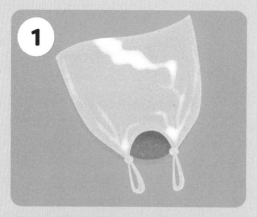

1

Tie knots in the handles of the shopping bag so that they leave a small hole for the hairdryer nozzle.

YOU WILL NEED:
- plastic shopping bag
- small plastic cup
- string
- small toy figure
- hairdryer

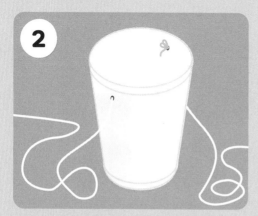

2

Ask an adult to help you attach some string to the plastic cup—this will be your basket.

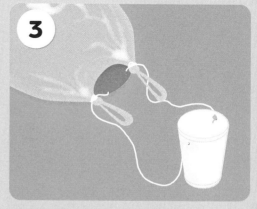

3

Tie the plastic cup to the handles of your shopping bag.

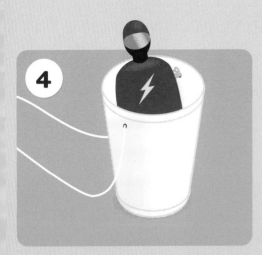

Put your toy figure inside the plastic cup, so they're ready for the ride!

Ask an adult to help you put the hairdryer nozzle into the small opening in the bag and blow in a little hot air.

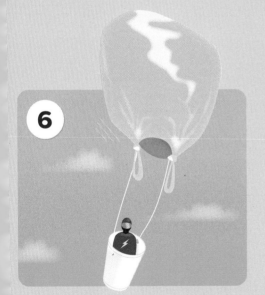

When the plastic bag is fully inflated, let it go, but keep the hairdryer running for a few more seconds. How far does your balloon travel?

WHY IT WORKS

When your bag is fully inflated it should rise upward. This is because the air inside the bag has been warmed by the hairdryer. The warm air is less dense than the cooler air around it because the air molecules are moving faster and farther apart. This causes your "balloon" to rise. The moving air from your hairdryer also gives the "balloon" a little lift!

MAKE A DECORATED CLAY POT

Dorothy and her friends come across a country where everything is made from china clay. Try making your own clay pot and decorating it!

1

Roll your clay into a ball about the size of the palm of your hand.

YOU WILL NEED:

- air-drying clay
- waterproof mat (or other protective surface)
- acrylic paints
- glue

2

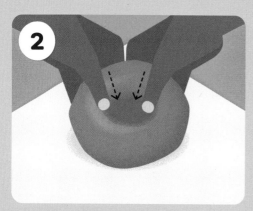

Put the clay on your mat and use your two thumbs to make an indentation in the middle.

3

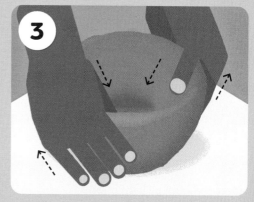

As you push downward, keep pulling the sides of your clay pot upward, to create a pot shape. Use your fingers to smooth the edges.

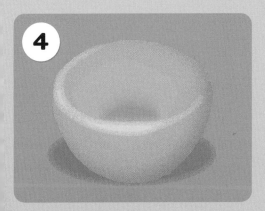

4

Let your clay pot dry for a day or two (this type of clay dries best when left to dry, rather than using a source of heat).

5

Paint your clay pot when it's dry. You can decorate it however you like. You may need two coats of paint.

6

Once dry, you can use your clay pot to store all kinds of things!

WHY IT WORKS

Clay has been used to make pottery and porcelain for many thousands of years. Clay can be found in the ground, usually where streams or rivers once flowed. Clay is a useful material because it can be molded when moist. When the clay is left to dry (or "fired" in an oven), the water evaporates and it becomes rock-hard.

Chapter 10

Glinda Grants Dorothy's Wish

As they walked through the china country, they had to take care not to knock anyone over. It took an hour or so to reach the china wall on the other side. It was smaller this time and they all managed to scramble to the top by standing on the Lion's back. As the Lion leapt onto the wall, he knocked over a china church with his tail and smashed it to pieces.

"That's too bad," said Dorothy, "but I really think we were lucky we didn't do more harm."

On the other side, they crossed a marshy bog before coming to a forest, where the trees were bigger and older than any they'd ever seen. "This is delightful," said the Lion, looking around joyfully. "I should like to live here all my life."

They walked on until it was too dark to go any farther and settled for the night. The next morning, they'd not gone far when they heard a low rumble. They came to an opening, where hundreds of beasts had gathered. There were tigers, elephants, bears, and wolves, among others, and for a moment Dorothy was afraid.

When the beasts caught sight of the Lion, they grew quiet. A tiger came up and said, "Welcome, King of the Beasts! You've come in good time to fight our enemy."

"What's your trouble?" asked the Lion quietly.

"We're all threatened by a most tremendous monster," answered the tiger, "like a great spider, with a body as big as an elephant. It uses its eight long legs to seize an animal and drag it to its mouth to eat, like a spider does a fly. None of us are safe."

"If I put an end to your enemy, will you obey me as King of the Forest?" the Lion asked.

"We'll do that gladly," replied the tiger, and all the other beasts roared, "We will!"

"Take care of my friends," said the Lion, "and I'll go at once."

Before long, the Lion returned to the beasts and said proudly, "You need fear your enemy no longer." He promised to come back and rule once Dorothy was safely home.

When they came out from the forest's gloom, a steep hill rose before them, covered with great rocks. They'd nearly reached the first rock when they heard a rough voice cry out, "Keep back!"

"Who are you?" asked the Scarecrow. Then a head showed itself over the rock. "This hill belongs to us, and we don't allow anyone to cross it."

"But we're going to the Land of the Quadlings," said the Scarecrow.

STRENGTH OF SPIDER SILK

Spiders use a sticky silk to spin a web to catch their prey. They also use a type of "drag line" silk to move between different surfaces. This silk is strong enough to hold their body's weight. The strongest silk comes from the Golden Orb-Weaver spider.

Drag line silk is 1,000 times thinner than a human hair but about five times stronger than steel of the same thickness. It can also be stretched several times its length before it breaks.

In ancient times, spider silk was used to bandage wounds and for fishing lines or nets. While it can be difficult to farm spider silk in large quantities (spiders tend to eat each other!), scientists are looking at ways to make artificial spider silk that could be used in construction and medicine.

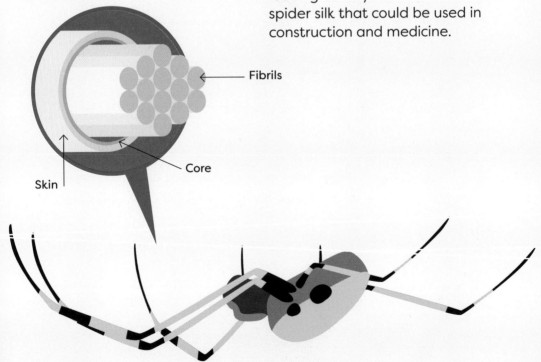

Fibrils

Core

Skin

"You can't!" replied the voice, and out stepped the strangest man the travelers had ever seen.

He was short and stout and had a big head, which was flat at the top and supported by a thick, wrinkly neck. He had no arms at all, which made the Scarecrow think he couldn't possibly prevent them from passing, as he walked on boldly.

As quick as lightning, the man's head shot forward and his neck stretched until the top of his flat head struck the Scarecrow and sent him tumbling down. The man laughed harshly.

A chorus of boisterous laughter came from the other rocks and Dorothy saw hundreds of armless Hammer-Heads behind every rock on the hillside. The Lion was angry and dashed up the hill, giving a loud roar. But again, a head shot swiftly out, and struck him down.

"What can we do?" Dorothy asked.

"Call the Winged Monkeys," suggested the Tin Man. "You still have one more wish."

Dorothy wore the Golden Cap and uttered the magic words. "What do you command?" the Monkey King asked.

THE NUMBER THREE

There is something magical about the number three. Have you ever heard the phrases "third time lucky," "three of a kind," or "things happen in threes"?

The number three is all around us. In physics, there are three types of charge (positive, negative, and neutral), three particles in atoms (protons, neutrons, and electrons) and three states of matter (solid, liquid, and gas). We see things in three-dimensions (height, width, and depth) and we divide time into past, present, and future.

Three-sided shapes are very strong (see page 141). You can squash a square but a triangle stands firm. There are lots of triangles in nature, such as the shape of a mountain, a shark's fin, the center of a cucumber, or a three-leafed clover. Look around and you'll be amazed how many things rely on the number three!

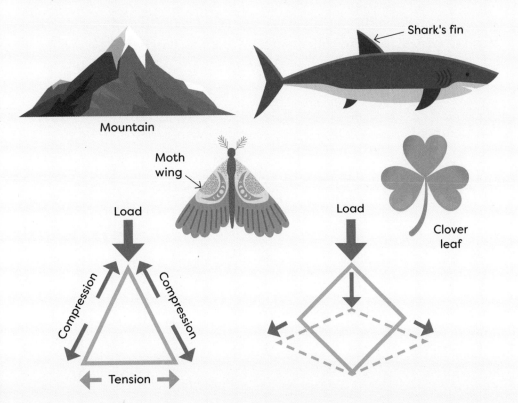

Shark's fin

Mountain

Moth wing

Clover leaf

Load

Compression

Compression

Tension

Load

"Carry us to the country of the Quadlings," Dorothy replied. At once, they were on their way and soon set down in a beautiful country.

"That was your last wish," said the Monkey King. "Goodbye, and good luck." The Monkeys flew out of sight.

The Land of the Quadlings had fields of grain, well-paved roads, and rippling brooks. The fences and houses were all red and the Quadlings dressed in red, too. They were good-natured, short, and rather chubby.

It wasn't long before they came across a beautiful castle, guarded by three girls dressed in red. One went to inform Glinda, who said they should be admitted at once.

Glinda sat upon a throne of rubies. She was beautiful and young, with rich red hair that fell in ringlets. Her dress was pure white, and her eyes were blue. "What can I do for you, my child?" she asked kindly.

Dorothy told the Witch her story: how the tornado had brought her to the Land of Oz, and of the wonderful adventures they'd all had.

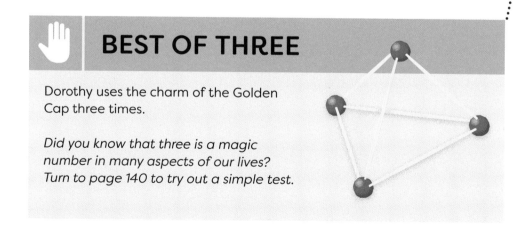

BEST OF THREE

Dorothy uses the charm of the Golden Cap three times.

Did you know that three is a magic number in many aspects of our lives? Turn to page 140 to try out a simple test.

"My greatest wish now," she said, "is to get back to Kansas. Aunt Em must be worrying about me."

Glinda kissed Dorothy. "Bless your dear heart," she said, "I'm sure I can help you. But if I do, you must give me the Golden Cap."

"Gladly!" cried Dorothy. "It's no use to me now."

The Witch asked the Scarecrow, "What will you do when Dorothy's left us?" "I'll return to the Emerald City," he replied, "for Oz has made me its ruler. I'm not sure how to cross the Hammer-Heads, though."

"I shall tell the Winged Monkeys to carry you there," said Glinda. "It would be a shame to deprive the people of so wonderful a ruler."

Turning to the Tin Man, she asked, "What will become of you when Dorothy leaves us?"

"The Winkies were very kind and want me to rule over them," he replied. "But I would have to get back to the Country of the West."

"I shall command the Winged Monkeys to take you to the land of the Winkies," said Glinda, "I'm sure you'll rule them wisely."

Then the Witch looked at the Lion and asked, "When Dorothy returns home, what will become of you?"

"Over the hill of the Hammer-Heads," the Lion replied, "lies an old forest, where all the beasts have made me their King. If I could get back there, I'd be very happy."

"I shall command the Winged Monkeys to carry you there," Glinda said. "Then having used up the powers of the Golden Cap, I'll give it to the Monkey King, to free them forever."

The Scarecrow, Tin Man, and Lion thanked the Good Witch for her kindness. "You're as good as you are beautiful!" Dorothy exclaimed, "but how do I get back to Kansas?"

"Your silver shoes will carry you there," Gilda replied. "If you'd known their power, you could have gone back the first day you came here."

"But then I wouldn't have had my wonderful brains!" cried the Scarecrow. "And I wouldn't have had my lovely heart," said the Tin Man. "And I'd have lived a coward forever," declared the Lion.

"This is true," said Dorothy, "and I'm glad to have helped you. But now you're all happy with a kingdom to rule, I'd like to go back to Kansas."

POWERFUL WINGS

The Winged Monkeys use their strong wings to carry Dorothy's friends back to their kingdoms.

Can you make a monkey with flapping wings? Turn to page 142 for a guide.

"Just knock the heels together three times," Glinda explained, "and command the shoes to carry you wherever you wish to go."

Dorothy threw her arms around the Lion's neck and kissed him. Then she kissed the Tin Man and hugged the soft body of the Scarecrow and found she was crying too.

Dorothy thanked Glinda and said one last goodbye. She clapped her heels together three times, "Take me home to Aunt Em!"

Instantly, she was whirling through the air. The silver shoes took three steps, and then stopped so suddenly that she rolled on the grass. "Good gracious!" Dorothy cried as she sat up.

She was sitting on the broad Kansas prairie in front of the new farmhouse Uncle Henry had built. Then Dorothy realized the silver shoes had fallen off in her flight and were lost in the desert forever.

When Aunt Em came out of the house, she saw Dorothy running toward her. "My darling child!" she cried, folding the little girl in her arms. "Where in the world did you come from?"

"From the Land of Oz," said Dorothy gravely. "And here is Toto, too. Oh, Aunt Em! I'm *so* glad to be home again!"

THE END

MAKE A PYRAMID

Dorothy can use the charm of the Golden Cap three times. Try this experiment to see how the number three is a magical number.

1

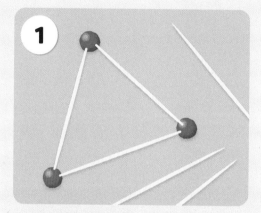

Use three toothpicks to make a triangle. Use blobs of playdough to join the points together.

YOU WILL NEED:

- 14 toothpicks
- playdough

2

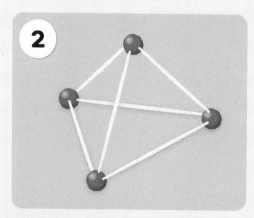

Now add a toothpick to each blob of playdough. Bring them together at the top to make a triangle-based pyramid.

3

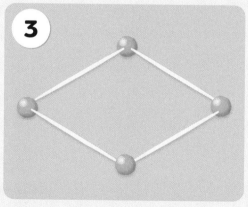

This time use four toothpicks to make a square, using blobs of playdough to join the points together.

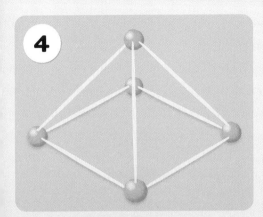

4 Add a toothpick to each blob of playdough and bring them together at the top to make a square-based pyramid.

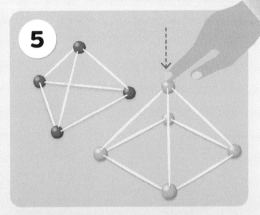

5 Press down gently on each shape. Which shape is stronger? Why do you think this is?

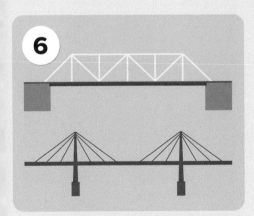

6 Try to think of examples of squares and triangles in different structures around you. Why do you think both squares and triangles are used?

WHY IT WORKS

Triangles are very strong shapes. Squares have useful horizontal and vertical sides but they can become squashed or distorted. A triangle stands firm because you cannot change a triangle's shape without changing the length of one of its sides. You can turn a square into two triangles by putting a line diagonally through the middle. This makes it a popular shape in construction.

MAKE A WINGED MONKEY

The Winged Monkeys fly across the land carrying out the wishes of the Golden Cap. Try making a monkey of your own and watch its wings flap!

1

Draw a large monkey-shape on your paper. You can use this template as a guide.

YOU WILL NEED:

- sheet of printer paper
- pencil and markers
- scissors
- tape
- thin pipe cleaner
- paper straw

2

Cut out the monkey and color it in.

3

Ask an adult to help you cut a small slit in the middle of the monkey.

Push the pipe cleaner gently through the slit from the back to the front. Bend on the other side and secure with tape.

Cut a slit in the straw, about halfway up. Thread the straw over your pipe cleaner and tape down a slit on each wing.

Now you can move your straw up and down, to flap your monkey's wings!

WHY IT WORKS

When you tape your straw to the monkey's wings, it acts as a hinge. Pulling up on the straw lifts the monkey's wings, and pushing down on the straw moves them back again. The pipe cleaner acts as a supporting handle.